Open Windows

Open Windows

Philip Yancey

CROSSWAY BOOKS • WESTCHESTER, ILLINOIS
A DIVISION OF GOOD NEWS PUBLISHERS

Some of the writing in this book has appeared, in different form, in
Christianity Today, Leadership and the *Christian Century*. The chapter
"Pitfalls of Christian Writing" grew out of ideas that originally appeared
in *Publishers Weekly*.

The publisher and author express appreciation for permission to quote
from the following:

Four Quartets by T. S. Eliot, taken from *Collected Poems 1909-1962*,
copyright © 1963; used by permission of Harcourt Brace Jovanovich, Inc.

Pilgrim at Tinker Creek (Pulitzer Prize winner, a Harper's Magazine Press
book) and *Holy the Firm* by Annie Dillard, copyright © 1974 and 1977
respectively; used by permission of Harper & Row.

First printing, 1982

Printed in the United States of America.
Library of Congress Catalog Card Number: 82-71879
ISBN: 0-89107-256-X

To Janet, my wife,
who fills the word love with meaning

Contents

PART ONE

A Little Leaven

My personal introduction to the concentration camps came during a late-night conversation in the Albany, New York, home of a Jewish photographer. Many of his relatives had perished under Hitler's "Final Solution," and he was then experiencing the second-generation symptoms later explored by Helen Epstein in Children of the Holocaust. *The scenes he described, passed down from great-aunts and -uncles, horrified me.*

Later the laconic prose of Elie Wiesel and the angry blasts of Solzhenitsyn pulled me into the great body of literature that spun out centrifugally from the camps. What I found in the accounts surprised me. The enslaved millions formed a separate civilization, a compression of basic humanity stripped of its normal trappings. Survivors teach us as much about life outside the camps as about life inside.

An appalling number of people today have no knowledge of (or interest in) the lessons from the concentration camps. To me, this sense of polite apathy is the worst injustice we can grant the few survivors. We owe them far more.

CHAPTER ONE

Lessons from the Camps

NEWSCASTER Edward R. Murrow, covering the Allied troops' liberation of Germany, accompanied one of the first contingents to overtake a German concentration camp. No American was prepared for the horrible scene within the gates: emaciated, bony corpses stacked like cordwood and the awful stench of burning flesh. Worst of all were the living corpses, the *Muselmanner*, or walking dead. One man, a human skeleton with skin draped over him like loose-fitting leather, stared at Murrow with haunting, empty eyes. Finally he spoke in a raspy, wheezing voice: "Mr. Murrow . . . Mr. Murrow . . . do you remember me?"

Edward R. Murrow glanced at the man and quickly shook his head. But the man persisted. He grabbed Murrow's arm in his clawlike fingers and said, "Don't you remember? You interviewed me in Prague. I was the mayor then, of Prague, Czechoslovakia."

Six years after that liberation, thousands of miles away in the desolate Siberian wasteland, Aleksandr Solzhenitsyn was serving out his term for making a disparaging reference to Stalin in a letter. After six gloomy years he suddenly discovered the joy of writing. "Sometimes in a sullen work party with Tommy-gunners barking about me, lines and images crowded in so urgently that I felt myself borne through the air, overleaping the column in my hurry to reach the work site and find a corner to write. At such moments I was both free and happy" (*Gulag III*, p. 99).

But how could he write? Any scrap of paper would be confiscated and cause suspicion against him, no matter how innocent the writings were. After all, the lines could be in code or perhaps contain the membership list of some organization. Solzhenitsyn learned that a prisoner's memory, cleansed of superfluous knowledge, was surprisingly capacious. He would write down snatches of twelve to twenty lines at a time, polish them, learn them by heart, and burn them. Then to keep count, he started breaking matches into little pieces and arranging them in two rows of ten each. As he recited the verses to himself, he would remove one bit of broken match from each row, first counting units, then tens of lines. Even this had to be done with care, for the regular moving of match bits along with the whispering movements of lips could have aroused stool pigeons' suspicions. Every fiftieth and hundredth line Solzhenitsyn memorized with special care, to help him keep count. Once a month he recited everything he had written. If the fiftieth or hundredth lines came out wrong, he would painstakingly go over and over the lines until he had them right.

Later, observing Lithuanian Catholics with their rosaries, Solzhenitsyn decided their counting technique would be more practical. He made a rosary of one hundred colored pieces of hardened bread, every tenth piece cubic. Amazing the Lithuanians with his religious zeal (devout ones possessed only forty beads) he happily fingered and counted beads inside his wide mittens—standing in lineups, marching to work, at all waiting times. Warders who discovered the beads assumed they were for praying and let him keep the necklace.

By the end of his sentence Solzhenitsyn had accumulated twelve thousand lines, which upon release he eagerly committed to paper.

As does every generation, ours is haltingly trying to come to terms with its recent past. The concentration camps, notably those erected by Hitler and Stalin (Little Moustache and Big

Moustache, as Solzhenitsyn calls them), caused such a moral crater in the history of humanity that only now are we beginning to absorb and assess their impact. In recent years events such as the television series *The Holocaust* and the publication of Solzhenitsyn's monumental three-volume work *The Gulag Archipelago* have stirred the consciousness of the general public.

The psychic effect of German concentration camps has been well documented by psychologist-survivors Viktor Frankl, Bruno Bettelheim, and Elie Cohen and powerfully retold by such novelists as Elie Wiesel and John Hersey. Because of strict censorship, accounts of Soviet camps have been more sporadic and deficient, and until Solzhenitsyn no one had been able to compile any kind of a thorough history. If Germany's genocidal camps left a scar across the body of all humanity, Stalin's camps inflicted a near-fatal wound stretching across the breadth of the Soviet Union. Best estimates are that sixty million were killed or incarcerated by Stalin. Of these, fifteen million died in the great plague of enforced starvation and disease in the Ukraine. That means one in three Soviet citizens lost a family member to the terror of Stalin's reign.

Why spotlight attention on concentration camps? Though it may cause discomfort and even anguish, such attention serves several useful functions. The primary function is chiseled into stone at the Dachau memorial, as articulated by philosopher Santayana, "Those who cannot remember the past are condemned to repeat it." We who have been reared in a climate of existential despair cannot fathom the optimistic belief in human progress that crescendoed before World War I and was finally put to death in Germany and in Russia. The two great fonts of culture and civilization (*Christian* civilization) gave birth to demonic forces. The camps became the central metaphor of evil in all history, so much so that George Bernard Shaw reluctantly concluded, "There is only one empirically verifiable doctrine of theology—original sin."

There is no way to exaggerate the impact of the camps on the modern view of humanity. Deliberate cruelty had become institutionalized as official state policy. Predictions that the world is "getting better and better every day in every way" abruptly stopped.

Historians sorting through the archives of the Third Reich came across such words as these, spoken by Heinrich Himmler to SS generals at Posen in 1943: "I also want to talk to you quite frankly on a very grave matter. Among ourselves it should be mentioned quite frankly, and yet we will never speak of it publicly . . . I mean . . . the extermination of the Jewish race . . . Most of *you* know what it means when 100 corpses are lying side by side, or 500, or 1,000. To have stuck it out and at the same time—apart from exceptions caused by human weakness—to have remained decent fellows, that is what has made us hard. This is a page of glory in our history which has never been written and is never to be written . . ." (*Rise and Fall of the Third Reich*, p. 1259).

Words like *inhuman* and *unconscionable* were voided of meaning by the SS programs, which had, in fact, been carried out by humans who claimed their consciences were unaffected.

Anyone who has been sheltered from such horrors need only visit one of the preserved death camps, such as Auschwitz. There, in an open field, one can see flowers and grasses growing with unusual lushness. Bending down, one notices the white, powdery character of the soil that allows such fecund growth. The top twelve inches of that soil is fine bone loam—the remains of sixty thousand humans destroyed in the ovens of a single camp.

Jewish groups who worked for the preservation of such camps adopted the slogan "Never Again." Today the camps, cleaned up, well planted, seeming almost like state parks to the modern visitor, stand as an ineradicable testimony to the basic tragic flaw in humanity and a terrifying warning to all of us who may underestimate the evil bent of power.

The iron commitment of "Never Again" is the primary function of looking at the camps. They should have seared all humanity against the promises of totalitarianism. The long litany of evil which followed has proved the world's memory to be short indeed.

Yet the memory of the camps and of the men who created them is not the only lesson for us to learn. There are also the survivors: Solzhenitsyn, methodically laying his bricks in Siberian winters while thousands of lines danced in his head, the mayor of Prague, the psychologists Bettelheim and Frankl, the concert violinists—of the millions a few have endured to tell us about ourselves. Their voices are sometimes loud and screechy, even strident. Flannery O'Connor was once asked why she chose to write about odd, abnormal characters. Her reply: "To the near blind I write large. To the deaf I shout." Similarly, the survivors are caricatures of humanity forced to live in unbearable conditions; yet in such circumstances they reveal much about our ground of being. For there, in the camps, all distinguishing marks between prisoners were obliterated. To his captors Solzhenitsyn was just one more *zek* (Russian word for prisoner) with his head shaven and a number painted across his chest; to all the rest he was merely a competitor for food and space. Taken together, the prisoners, stripped of their individual identities, teach us about the nature of humanity.

At first glance, the lesson from the survivors seems predictable. On one side of the fence was an indistinguishable herd of prisoners, thrown together like animals in pens, every detail of their lives determined for them. On the other side were the guards, individuals free to attend concerts, work at their hobbies, practice their sports, read books, develop their characters. As Terrence Des Pres has pointed out, the aim of the camps was "to reduce inmates to mindless creatures whose behavior could be predicted and controlled absolutely. The camps have so far been the closest thing on earth to a perfect [B. F.] Skinner Box. They were a closed, completely regulated environment, a 'total' world in the strict sense. Pain and death were the 'negative reinforcers,' food and life the 'positive reinforcers,' and all these forces were pulling and shoving twenty-four hours a day at the deepest stratum of human need" (*The Survivor*, p. 162).

The experiment failed. A "rehabilitated" Solzhenitsyn cried out so loudly he was expelled from his homeland. Many men and women who survived the German camps resumed their normal lives, scarred and bruised by the experience, yes, but far from becoming the mindless robots wished for by their captors. If you visit a dinner held by survivors of the camps in memory of their experience, you will find doctors, lawyers, businessmen— nearly a cross section of humanity in general. They include children who were raised under a regime that approached absolute evil; yet even within them one often finds a highly developed morality and compassion for humanity.

Writings of the survivors sing with detailed character studies of individuals. A simple, brief book like Solzhenitsyn's *One Day in the Life of Ivan Denisovich*, which limits its scope to one sixteen-hour period in one camp, contains a wealth of three-dimensional portraits of inmates.

In one sense the camps reduce people to purely materialistic beings. The only things that matter, really, are the bowl of warm soup with the greasy fishbones floating in it, and the pair of felt boots and warm mittens. Eight ounces of bread is the minimum—more for those who work hard. However, it soon becomes obvious to anyone who reads the survivors' accounts that they are not the accounts of materialistic beings. Though every vestige of food for the human spirit has been carefully removed, still, the spirit surges up. Within the malnourished bodies of the inmates there is a highly developed sense of *morality, art,* and *hope.* None of those qualities are to be expected in such a place. Yet they spring up like fountains out of granite.

(I should note here that by necessity I must generalize from a variety of accounts by the survivors. Of course there was crude violence, inhumanity, conniving, and cruelty among the inmates. There was also mindless obedience, in many cases. These are to be expected. What is remarkable, however, is that in an environment designed to breed such responses, other, more lofty signs of humanity appeared at all. I should also note that I am mostly talking of concentration camps, not death camps. The death camps, where each new entrant knew he or she had only days to live, produced an extraordinary set of pressures. As Elie Wiesel has tragically described in his remembrances, death camps included such scenes as sons beating their fathers to death for a piece of bread. Even there, however, glimpses of compassion and self-sacrifice existed, as Wiesel himself showed in his loving concern for his father.)

If the victims reveal a surprising degree of individuality and resilience, their captors in almost all accounts blur together into an amorphous, indistinguishable clot. Solzhenitsyn realized this when he arose to address a special committee inquiring into certain prisoners' complaints. "All that is written in these pages, all that we had gone through, all that we had brooded over in all those years and all those days on hunger strike—I might as well try telling it to orangutans as to them. They were still in some formal sense Russians, still more or less capable of understanding fairly simple Russian phrases, such as 'Permission to enter!,' 'Permission to speak, sir!' But as they sat there all in a row at the long table, exhibiting their sleek, white, complacent, uniformly blank physiognomies, it was plain that they had long ago degenerated into a distinct biological type, that verbal communication between us had broken down beyond repair, and that we could exchange only . . . bullets" (*Gulag III*, p. 267).

Another witness, George Mangakis, described the process of his torturer becoming the real victim after he was imprisoned during the Greek junta in the late 1960s.

I have experienced the fate of a victim. I have seen the torturer's face at close quarters. It was in a worse condition than my own bleeding, livid face. The torturer's face was distorted by a kind of twitching that had nothing human about it. . . . In this situation, I turned out to be the lucky one. I was humiliated. I did not humiliate others. I was simply bearing a profoundly unhappy humanity in my aching entrails. Whereas the men who humiliate you must first humiliate the notion of humanity within themselves. Never mind if they strut around in their uniforms, swollen with the knowledge that they can control the suffering, sleeplessness, hunger, and despair of their fellow human beings, intoxicated with the power in their hands. Their intoxication is nothing other than the degradation of humanity. The ultimate degradation. They have had to pay very dearly for my torments.

I wasn't the one in the worst position. I was simply a man who moaned because he was in great pain. I prefer that. At this moment I am deprived of the joy of seeing children going to school or playing in the parks. Whereas they have to look their own children in the face.

Morality
Among the prisoners, a sense of morality persisted even in an environment of near absolute evil. It is true, some survivors lost their faith in God. Jews, especially, were susceptible: raised to believe they had been chosen people, they suddenly discovered that, as one Jew poignantly expressed, "Hitler is the only one who has kept his promises, all his promises, to the Jewish people."

Elie Wiesel records a true and profoundly moving episode which occurred while he, at age fifteen, was imprisoned at Buna. In one scene it expresses the horror of the camps perhaps more potently than all the camp statistics ever published.

A cache of arms had been discovered at the camp, belonging to a Dutchman, who was promptly shipped to Auschwitz. But the Dutchman had a young boy who served him, a *pipel* as they were called, a child with a refined and beautiful face, unheard of in the camps. He had the face of a sad angel.

The little servant, like his Dutch master, was cruelly tortured, but would not reveal any information. So the SS sentenced him to death, along with two other prisoners who had been discovered with arms.

One day when we came back from work, we saw three gallows rearing up in the assembly place, three black crows. Roll call. SS all round us, machine guns trained: the traditional ceremony. Three victims in chains—and one of them, the little servant, the sad-eyed angel.

The SS seemed more preoccupied, more disturbed than usual. To hang a young boy in front of thousands of spectators was no light matter. The head of the camp read the verdict. All eyes were on the child. He was lividly pale, almost calm, biting his lips. The gallows threw its shadow over him.

This time the Lagerkapo refused to act as executioner. Three SS replaced him.

The three victims mounted together onto the chairs.

The three necks were placed at the same moment within the nooses.

"Long live liberty!" cried the two adults.

But the child was silent.

"Where is God? Where is He?" someone behind me asked.

At a sign from the head of the camp, the three chairs tipped over.

Total silence throughout the camp. On the horizon, the sun was setting.

"Bare your heads!" yelled the head of the camp. His voice was raucous. We were weeping.

"Cover your heads!"

Then the march past began. The two adults were no longer alive. Their tongues hung swollen, blue-tinged. But the third rope was still moving; being so light, the child was still alive. . . .

For more than half an hour he stayed there, struggling between life and death, dying in slow agony under our eyes. And we had to look him full in the face. He was still alive when I passed in front of him. His tongue was still red, his eyes were not yet glazed.

Behind me, I heard the same man asking: "Where is God now?"

And I heard a voice within me answer him: "Where is He? Here He is—He is hanging here on this gallows. . . ."

That night the soup tasted of corpses (*Night*, pp. 75-76).

Wiesel lost his faith in God at that concentration camp. But not because he lost belief in morality—for the opposite reason. He believed in morality so deeply that he could no longer worship a God who would allow children to be strung up at the gallows and tossed into the ovens.

The lesson intended by the SS guards at Buna was to reinforce their imposed justice: cooperate, and you may live; resist, and you will surely die. But the effect on the prisoners was just the opposite. Hardened as they were by viewing thousands of deaths, the prisoners convulsed before this one. The object lesson did nothing to break the spirit of resistance; it merely stiffened the will of those who were determined somehow to strike out against their tormentors.

Who survived the camps? The people who cooperated with guards, informing on fellow prisoners? Not in Germany. According to Bruno Bettelheim, "Those who . . . made common cause with the enemy, the camp commander, thus sacrificing the lives of others to gain advantages for themselves, were not likely to remain alive. The prisoners, to survive, had to help one another."

In Russia, too, prisoners constructed their own scheme of morality. Some of it was brutal. Stool pigeons, for example, were not tolerated—their throats were slit in the night. But when prisoners succeeded in taking over an entire camp at Kengir for six weeks, they set up humane and workable rules to govern themselves—far more sensible than those rules imposed by the guards. They did not disintegrate into anarchy and greed even when power and a measure of freedom were suddenly thrust upon them.

Psychologists who have studied concentration camp survivors universally affirm that guilt is one of the chief residual effects. Guilt over why they, and not others, survived. Guilt over whether they did enough to protest. As Bettelheim confesses, "The survivor as a thinking being knows very well that he is not guilty, as I, for one, know about myself, but this does not change the fact that the humanity of such a person, as a feeling being, requires that he *feel* guilty, and he does. This is a most significant aspect of survivorship." Elie Wiesel writes, "I live and therefore I am guilty. I am still here, because a friend, a comrade, an unknown died in my place."

It is perhaps the ultimate irony that German after German calmly marched to the stand at Nuremburg to report that he felt no guilt about what had been done to the Jews, that he was "just following orders." Meanwhile scores of thousands of innocent people inherited an intolerable burden of guilt because their sense of morality would not dissolve inside the camps.

From his experience in the camps, Solzhenitsyn did not conclude that all inmates were pure and just, or even that all guards were viciously evil. But, as he records in the second volume of *Gulag*, his view of humanity was profoundly altered by what he saw in the camps: "It was only when I lay there on rotting prison straw that I sensed within myself the first stirrings of good. Gradually it was disclosed to me that the line separating good and evil passes not through states, nor between classes, nor between political parties either—but right through every human heart—and through all human hearts. . . . *Bless you, prison*, for having been in my life" (p. 615).

The Psalmist cried out: "Where can I flee from your presence? If I go up to the heavens you are there; if I make my bed in the depths, you are there" (Psalm 139:8, NIV).

God has stamped his image upon us so indelibly that we can also add: the image of God in human beings is inescapable. In the depths of depraved human hell, in the presence of absolute evil, even there glimpses of it can be found. The concentration camps teach us the depravity of humankind, surely. But they also hint at our immortality.

Art

Although nearly every element of what is generally known as art or culture had been dismantled within the camps, this human expression, too, kept asserting itself. There were fewer reminders of art, to be sure—no concerts or ballets, and few books allowed. But the inmates carried within them memories and a highly developed aesthetic sense. Even when life was reduced to its raw basics, when art required an exertion that might rob from the more pressing needs of survival, it surfaced.

Eugenie Ginzburg, a Communist Party activist who fell into disfavor and spent two decades in one of the worst Gulag camps, remembered it this way: "During those years I experienced many conflicting feelings, but the dominant one was that of amazement. . . . We still took pleasure in the fugitive mists of morning, the violet sunsets that blazed over us as we returned from the quarry, the proximity of ocean-going ships which we felt by some sixth sense—and in poetry, which we still repeated to one another at night. . . . I felt instinctively that as long as I could be stirred to emotion by the sea breeze, by the brilliance of the stars, and by poetry, I would still be alive, however much my legs might tremble and my back bend under the load of burning stones."

For Solzhenitsyn, as has been mentioned, writing became the single force which allowed him to leap over the walls of the camp. His body, still stuffed into a *zek* uniform, went through the exhausting daily regimen of wake-up calls, hard labor, food lines. But in the pause between wheelbarrowloads of mortar, in the winter warming-up shack, on the scaffolding, he would furtively scribble down new verses which filled his head.

"I lived in a dream," he says, "I sat in the mess hall over the ritual gruel sometimes not even noticing its taste, deaf to those around me—feeling my way about my verses and trimming them to fit like bricks in a wall. I was searched, and counted, and herded over the steppe—and all the time I saw the sets for my play, the color of the curtains, the placing of the furniture, the spotlights, every movement of the actors across the stage.

"Some of the lads broke through the wire in a lorry, others crawled under it, others walked up a snowdrift and over it—but for me the wire might not have existed; all this time I was making my own long and distant escape journey, and this was something the warders could not discover when they counted heads" (*Gulag III*, p. 104).

Across the Gulag, and in the camps in Germany, how many

countless others were stirred like Solzhenitsyn? How many invented their own secret codes and elaborate techniques for hiding their writings from the guards, and took those codes to the grave with them, silently?

The prisoners, cramped into unimaginably small spaces, given barely enough calories a day to subsist, even under such conditions found the energy for writing, for music, for art.

Sometimes books were available, and the prisoners paged through those precious objects as if each one was made of priceless parchment. Eugen Kogon, an author and survivor of Buchenwald, found a rare opportunity for quiet reading. In the winter of 1942 a series of bread thefts at Buchenwald made it necessary to establish a night watch. For months he volunteered for the extra shift, sitting alone from three to six o'clock in the morning. The only sounds were the snores of sleeping comrades. "What an experience it was," he reports, "to sit quietly by a shaded lamp, delving into the pages of Plato's *Dialogues*, Galsworthy's *Swan Song*, or the works of Heine, Klabund, Mehring!"

Elie Wiesel records a poignant scene that occurred when he and hundreds of other Jews were barracked for three days at Gleiwitz, pressed into a room so tightly that many smothered because the sheer mass of human bodies cut off all sources of air. Twisted among the bodies was an emaciated young Warsaw Jew named Juliek. Somehow, incredibly, Juliek had clutched his violin to him during the forced death march through snowstorms to Gleiwitz. That night, crammed among the hundreds of dead and nearly suffocating humans, Juliek struggled free and began to play a fragment from Beethoven's concerto. The sounds were pure, eldritch, misplaced in such a setting.

Wiesel recalls, "It was pitch dark. I could hear only the violin, and it was as though Juliek's soul were the bow. He was playing his life. The whole of his life was gliding on the strings—his lost hopes, his charred past, his extinguished future. He played as he would never play again. . . . To this day, whenever I hear Beethoven played my eyes close and out of the dark rises the sad, pale face of my Polish friend, as he said farewell on his violin to an audience of dying men.

"I do not know for how long he played. I was overcome by

sleep. When I awoke, in the daylight, I could see Juliek, opposite me, slumped over, dead. Near him lay his violin, smashed,
trampled, a strange overwhelming little corpse" (*Night*, pp. 107-
108).

To me, the scene Wiesel describes stands as a parable of the
role of art in the camps. There, death rules. All that is beautiful,
joyful, and worthy is removed. Yet the camps contain people,
not animals. And amid the shoving and scratching for existence
there emerges a rumor of transcendence: the pure, otherworldly
tone of a Beethoven violin concerto. From a pragmatic viewpoint, music, art, and poetry seem almost a mockery of the black
despair that weighed so heavily on the camps. Yet their existence proves that the human spirit dies as stubbornly as does the
body.

The most unexpectedly powerful lesson from the camps is the
immortality they reveal. The candle of the image of God im-
planted within us cannot be snuffed out—not even in the cold,
dreadful vacuum of evil where God himself seemed absent.

Hope

Pandora, the mythical first mortal to enter the world, brought
with her a box containing all the mortal ills. The last ill remaining after she opened the box was hope.

To the victims of concentration camps, on whom all mortal
evils seemed focused as if by the lens of a magnifying glass,
hope was sometimes the great destroyer. Why were there not
more Jewish uprisings such as the one in Warsaw? Partly because the Jews had too much hope. They could not believe that
such inhumanities as the gas chambers existed, despite the
rumors sweeping through the Jewish settlements. Elie Wiesel in
Night tells the story of Moche, an old Jew who miraculously
escaped the machine-gun slaughter of Jews near Kolomaye, Poland. He returned to Wiesel's small town in Hungary and went
from house to house warning his friends and neighbors of the
coming terror.

No one believed Moche. " 'They take me for a madman,' he
would whisper, and tears, like drops of wax, flowed from his
eyes."

Later, when Wiesel and his town's Jews were jammed into

railroad cars and hauled through blizzards toward Poland and Germany, another tried to warn them. Madame Schachter, a woman gone mad, would startle the boxcar occupants by standing at the window and shrieking, " 'Fire! Fire! . . . Jews, listen to me! I can see a fire! There are huge flames! It is a furnace!' "

No one listened to Madame Schachter either. Four different times she erupted with awful screams. Finally she was tied up in a corner and clubbed. The passengers could not stand the fear and tensions her outbursts caused. They had too much hope to believe the threats of a mad woman—until they pulled into Auschwitz and saw the chthonic flames for themselves.

Yet to the victims of the camps in Germany and Russia, hope was also the daily bread of survival. How can a man condemned to face twenty-five years of hard labor in Siberia make it through a day? He lowers his expectations, sets small goals and achievements for himself, anxiously searches for objects of hope. As Alyosha the Christian explained to Ivan Denisovich, he did not pray for packages or for extra stew or fur mittens. " 'Of all earthly and mortal things our Lord commanded us to pray only for our daily bread.' 'Give us this day our daily bread.' "

Solzhenitsyn's account of one day in the prisoner's life ends with Ivan falling asleep fully content. "He'd had many strokes of luck that day: they hadn't put him in the cells; they hadn't sent his squad to the settlement; he'd swiped a bowl of kasha at dinner; the squad leader had fixed the rates well; he'd built a wall and enjoyed doing it; he'd smuggled that bit of hacksaw blade through; he'd earned a favor from Tsezar that evening; he'd bought that tobacco. And he hadn't fallen ill. . . .

"A day without a dark cloud. Almost a happy day" (*One Day in the Life of Ivan Denisovich*, p. 158).

To those of us who spend our days worrying about excessive static on our car's FM radio, the worn pile on living-room carpets, and the decision of whether to add an extra layer of insulation in the attic, those hopes seem elemental indeed. But such is the nature of the human spirit. It adapts. And the great Solzhenitsyn, as well as the concert violinists, mayors, and artists shipped off to German and Russian camps, adapted downward. Their hopes became visceral and primordial.

Some survivors speak of "the puzzling potential of inner

strength" which permitted their bodies to keep warm though the penetrating chill froze the soil, and which allowed them to keep a cheerfulness of spirit while surrounded by death and extermination. Virtually all survivors firmly believed the Germans would lose the war, though they were surrounded by evidences of the Germans' strength.

The daily hope is not a foolish, Pollyanna belief that tables will soon be turned and all will be right. It is simply a decision, a mechanism of survival which feeds a will to live. Solzhenitsyn concludes, "All that the downtrodden can do is go on hoping. After every disappointment they must find fresh reason for hope." And they did.

In addition to this daily hope, however, there surfaced a deeper, more mysteriously uplifting hope—a hope for freedom.

How can any of us in America embrace the deep lust for freedom that fuels the inmates of concentration camps? We can read a thousand pages of Solzhenitsyn's accounts within the gray walls and then stumble upon his descriptions of those first few days outside. We can watch freedom-crazed Papillon, old and hobbled, as he dives off the one-hundred-foot cliff into the raging ocean. Or, perhaps, we can gaze on the freeze-frame on which the movie *Midnight Express* ends: Billy Hayes in his stolen guard uniform leaping for joy as he steps into the bright sunlight outside the brutal Turkish prison.

Freedom. To those visionaries who have felt it sucked from them, freedom is worth all enduring. To a committed escaper, two days outside the camp are worth any quantity of torture and beatings back inside.

Embarrassed, we wonder why Solzhenitsyn wags his finger at us, as he did at Harvard, for flaunting our freedom to the world and not caring enough to bring it to people who have been deprived.

Solzhenitsyn participated in one strangely defiant act of freedom: a hunger strike. That freedom was a self-inflicted punishment, but it was the only form of protest that could not be stopped. At least a man has control over whether he opens his mouth to keep alive.

"This was a hunger strike called not by well-fed people with reserves of subcutaneous fat, but by gaunt, emaciated men, who had felt the whip of hunger daily for years on end, who had achieved with difficulty some sort of physical equilibrium, and who suffered acute distress if they were deprived of a single 100-gram ration. Even the goners starved with the rest, although a three-day fast might tip them into irreversible and fatal decline. The food which we had refused, and which we had always thought so beggarly, was a mirage of plenty in the feverish dreams of famished men. . . .

"But there was a sort of satisfaction in this feeling of hopelessness. We had taken a futile, a desperate step, it could only end badly—and that was good. Our bellies were empty, our hearts were in our boots—*but some higher need was being satisfied*" (*Gulag III*, pp. 258-259).

Much later Solzhenitsyn participated in a new kind of freedom. He walked outside, his sentence completed.

"And off I *walk*! I wonder whether everybody knows the meaning of this great free word. I am walking along *by myself!* With no automatic rifles threatening me, from either flank or from the rear. I look behind me: no one there! If I like, I can take the right-hand side, past the school fence, where a big pig is rooting in a puddle. And if I like, I can walk on the left, where hens are strutting and scratching immediately in front of the District Education Department. . . .

"I cannot sleep! I walk and walk and walk in the moonlight. The donkeys sing their song. The camels sing. Every fiber in me sings: I am free! I am free!" (*Gulag III*, pp. 417, 42).

What is it that allows an Ivan Denisovich to go to bed fully content at night? What sparks a hunger strike by three hundred gaunt and starving men?

The experience of hope beyond all hoping, pregnant with symbolism, and the lust for freedom that burns inside the victims of the camp are further rumors of transcendence, evidences of the image of God stamped indelibly upon the human spirit. For God invested in humans such a potent dose of freedom that they ultimately perverted it to create the very camps which try to eliminate it.

Freedom has its abuses, of course. As C. S. Lewis said about democracy, we should seek it not because it is a romanticized ideal, but because we cannot entrust one person or a few with the precious gifts of power and freedom; we must spread them among the many.

One step beyond even the hope that expresses itself in a zeal for freedom is the religious hope that prevails among victims of the camps. "When things are bad," Solzhenitsyn said, "we are not ashamed of our God. We are only ashamed of Him when things go well."

Bruno Bettelheim, a psychologist and survivor of the camps, states flatly, "It is a well-known fact of the concentration camps that those who had strong religious and moral convictions managed life there much better than the rest. Their beliefs, including belief in an afterlife, gave them a strength to endure which was far above that of most others."

Demonstrating the same phenomenon, Terrence Des Pres quotes an unnamed survivor in his book *The Survivor*.

Pain and . . . fear . . . kept us awake. A cloudless sky, thickly set with glittering stars, looked in upon our grief-filled prison. The moon shone through the window. Its light was dazzling that night and gave the pale, wasted faces of the prisoners a ghostly appearance. It was as if all the life had ebbed out of them. I shuddered with dread, for it suddenly occurred to me that I was the only living man among corpses.

All at once the oppressive silence was broken by a mournful tune. It was the plaintive tones of the ancient "Kol Nidre" prayer. I raised myself up to see whence it came. There, close to the wall, the moonlight caught the uplifted face of an old man, who, in self-forgetful, pious absorption, was singing softly to himself. . . . His prayer brought the ghostly group of seemingly insensible human beings back to life. Little by little, they all roused themselves and all eyes were fixed on the moonlight-flooded face.

We sat up very quietly, so as not to disturb the old man, and he did not notice that we were listening. . . . When at last he was silent, there was exaltation among us, an exaltation which men can experience only when they have fallen as low as we had fallen and then, through the mystic power of a deathless prayer, have awakened once more the world of the spirit (*The Survivor*, pp. 92-93).

Religious hope did not survive for everyone. To some, the tragedy of the camps was final proof that God did not care about the human plight. But to others, in Stalin's Russia and Hitler's Germany, religious faith was a hope that could not be extinguished. Rumors of freedom and amnesties came and went: God could be hoped for forever, even though he seemed very distant at the time.

Resisting

We have surveyed some of the more remarkable effects of concentration camps on their victims. Contrary to expectations, the victims did not lose their identities and become faceless, docile automatons. Many showed individual acts of courage and self-sacrifice. Within them a highly developed sense of morality continued, so much so that they emerged with more of a gnawing sense of guilt than did their oppressors. Also, an appreciation for art and beauty flourished, even in the drab grayness of the camps.

Finally, a deep expression of hope and a lust for freedom characterized the victims. All of these point to the immortal human spirit. Unlike animals bred in a zoo, people never lose sight of their higher destiny. They never learn to *belong* to the camps.

Yet, that uplifting conclusion is far from satisfying. Solzhenitsyn emerged a stronger man—but what of his fellow *zeks* who died? Elie Wiesel today stirs the world's emotions with his memories of suffering—but what of the dead ones Wiesel describes? Six million Jews were killed; only one percent of that number were liberated from the camps.

And what of those who are permanently scarred? Some live with terror in their eyes, unable to cope with the outside world, incapable of trust. The sight of a German shepherd dog reduces them to trembling.

The message of *One Day in the Life of Ivan Denisovich* is that an iron will, some luck, and perhaps God can get you through one day in the concentration camps. But a larger question resounds. *Who will get you out?*

In the spring of 1978, while the TV series *The Holocaust* was being shown, my church introduced a service of identification for the Jews who had suffered, a Yom HaShoah liturgy for Christians. Various members of the congregation, including children, read us voices from the survivors: Chaim Kaplan's diary in the Warsaw ghetto, a child's poem about the lack of butterflies in the ghetto, Viktor Frankl's observations as a prison doctor, Elie Wiesel's poignant tales, Nelly Sach's poem about the crematorium chimneys, and a selection called "Why Do the Christians Hate Us?" from André Schwarz-Bart's novel *The Last of the Just*.

The congregation sat quietly while each of the readings was given. A few people had to leave when the descriptions became too graphic. A friend thoughtfully absorbed all that was said, and after the service gave me this reaction: "Something pains me more than all the agony and guilt I feel hearing those voices of the Jews. All I can do for them is empathize and feel sorry. What really bothers me is how many situations like that we are ignoring now. It's easy to blame the Christians in World War II for not acting quicker, more decisively. But are we reacting to-day—what about recent situations such as in Cambodia and Uganda? Should we be having services about those places in-stead?"

The facts of the Jewish concentration camps were published in great detail in advertisements in the *New York Times* as early as 1939. Yet few believed them, no one responded, and the United States did not even enter the war until two years later, after a direct attack by the Japanese.

Outside of Auschwitz, I have said, there is a field covered with twelve inches of fine bone loam, the remains of sixty thousand Jews burned there. Yet three million Cambodians were killed in our own day. How did we respond?

A tormenting question echoes and reechoes throughout the third volume of Solzhenitsyn's *Gulag Archipelago:* "Did I do enough to resist?" Survivors of the camps seem tortured with that issue. Yet to those of us on the outside, our attitude is seen in the fact that Harper and Row delayed publication of volume three for almost two years, because American readers had grown bored with Solzhenitsyn's descriptions of the camps, and volume two was not proving profitable.

Appeals for direct intervention in places like Uganda and Cambodia by the radical right, or even by people like Senator George McGovern, evoke either self-righteous indignation ("Didn't you learn from the experience of Vietnam?") or a pro-longed yawn. Who cares?

Yet it seems to me an unavoidable conclusion from the camps that one lesson is more important than all others: justice must come from the outside. All victims of a camp are apocalyptic—they can only wait for relief from an outside force. No amount of morality or courage, no sense of beauty or infection of hope, will assure their survival apart from the outside force. For the overwhelming majority, survival depends on the destruction of the concentration camp world. The main issue is not what the prisoners can do—they are impotent—but the need to overcome in some way the perpetrators of the camp.

Until the Allied liberation, of all the millions of Jews imprisoned, only three had managed to escape—the German camps were that efficient.

Solzhenitsyn uses the example of the Kengir camp rebellion as the dramatic keystone of his third volume. Did they do enough to resist? They took over the camp at Kengir for six weeks, tearing down walls, marrying women prisoners, establishing their own government and laws—all, of course, within the confines of the barbed-wire borders. Yet even Kengir lasted for just six weeks. Tanks and machine guns moved in, manifesting in a few tragic hours just how puny and futile that stirring attempt had been.

The cries of the survivors—Solzhenitsyn, Bettelheim, and the others—are so compelling one would expect them to unite a free world against tyranny of all forms. And yet the opposite is true. Jimmy Carter was scorned for foolishly trying to inject morality into foreign policy, daring to let issues of torture and human rights interfere with the more weighty matters of trade.

If today we uncovered genocide on the scale of the persecution of Jews by Nazi Germany, would we respond? Should we? To me, this is the complex, but inescapable issue that rises like a flame from the ruins of the concentration camps. And it is an issue we are politely ignoring. After reading dozens of accounts of the German and Russian tragedies, I have recoiled with indignation against the evil they comprise. Yet almost immediately, subtle forces enter in to soften the anger, soothe it away, ease me back to complacency. I have tried to identify those forces.

1. First, there is the simple fact that a person who is warm finds it hard to understand one who is cold. Solzhenitsyn him-

self, a bulwark of unflagging resistance against oppression, found this process seep into his consciousness after he gained respectability in the Khrushchev era and his novel *One Day in the Life of Ivan Denisovich* was printed by the national magazines. He was called into the opulent bureaucratic headquarters in Red Square to testify about the injustices he had seen and felt. He gave his report to understanding technocrats who had reasonable answers to all his protests. "And indeed," he records, "seen from this bright, festive room, from these comfortable armchairs, to the accompaniment of their smoothly flowing eloquence, the camps look not horrible but quite rational. . . . Well, would *you* let these terrible people loose on the community?" (*Gulag III*, p. 500).

Wary of the dangers of forgetting, Solzhenitsyn started an annual ritual on the anniversary of his arrest. He established "a *zek's* day": in the morning he cut off 650 grams of bread for his daily ration, and for lunch fixed himself some broth and a ladleful of thin mush. And, he reported, by the end of the day he "was already picking up crumbs to put in my mouth, and licking the bowl. The old sensations start up vividly."

This phenomenon of numbness to suffering took on terrible proportions shortly before World War II, as Joe Bayly pointed out in an *Eternity* magazine column. President Roosevelt and other world leaders met at Evian-les-Bains, France, in July of 1938 to discuss Hitler's encroachments on Austria and his maltreatment of Jews in Germany. Their efforts were futile. "More than any other factor," wrote one correspondent, the conference "underwrote the death warrant for six million European Jews."

That same correspondent, the Manchester *Guardian's* Peggy Mann, recently visited the resort area and talked to one employee who remembered the conference well. He recalled, "Very important people were here and all the delegates had a nice time. They took pleasure cruises on the lake. They gambled at night in the casino. They took mineral baths and massages at the *Establissement Thermal.* Some of them took the excursion to Chamonix to go summer skiing. Some went riding; we have, you know, one of the finest stables in France. Some played golf. We have a beautiful course overlooking the lake.

"Meetings? Yes, some attended the meetings. But, of course, it is difficult to sit indoors hearing speeches when all the pleasures that Evian offers are waiting outside."

The conference ended: immigration quotas were not changed to allow more Jews to escape to freedom, and Hitler was not censured.

And, I might add, it is difficult to sit indoors reading about the suffering and oppressed of the world when all the pleasures that America offers are waiting right outside.

2. Our resistance to fury at oppression has been aided, I think, by a mostly healthy reaction to our bumbling in Vietnam. Most people admit our policy there was mistaken in some way—either in conception or technique. Combining that experience with the one in Korea, we learned our nation cannot be policeman to the world. And now, as conflagrations flare around the world, especially in Central America and the Middle East, America takes a strident but muscleless posture. (The Soviet Union, of course, has cleverly gotten around the problem by paying our Cuban neighbors to the south to help carry out its foreign policy.)

Solzhenitsyn dares to hammer home at what he sees is the logical consequence of this reaction. In his Harvard speech he thundered,

The most cruel mistake occurred with the failure to understand the Vietnam War. Some people sincerely wanted all wars to stop just as soon as possible; others believed that there should be room for national, or Communist, self-determination in Vietnam, or in Cambodia, as we see today with particular clarity. But members of the U.S. anti-war movement wound up being involved in the betrayal of Far Eastern nations, in a genocide and in the suffering today imposed on 30 million people there. Do these convinced pacifists hear the moans coming from there? Do they understand their responsibility today? Or do they prefer not to hear? The American intelligentsia lost its nerve, and as a consequence thereof danger has come much closer to the United States. But there is no awareness of this. Your short-sighted politicians who signed the hasty Vietnam capitulation seemingly gave America a carefree breathing spell; however, a hundred-fold Vietnam now looms over you.

Solzhenitsyn drew those conclusions; I am not ready to. But I admit to being affected by a reaction against our country's fail-ures in the past. A dog bitten by a snake is less apt to chase snakes again.

3. A latent pacifism has gained ground in Christian circles, especially in Europe but increasingly now in America also.

In September of 1978, *Sojourners* magazine ran an article enti-tled "Security in a Nuclear World," by Gordon Cosby. In it Cosby argued that our dependence on spending billions for national defense is "a negation of biblical faith."

"One thing history confirms," he continues. "The nation who trusts in anything other than God is abandoned by God. Every attempt at security fails because God abandons that people. We feel that the danger of extinction is being held back by 9,500 missiles. They are not holding anything back. God in his mercy is holding it back. The missiles are the vials of his wrath waiting to be overturned. We would be safer without them."

I wondered why Rev. Cosby didn't apply the same logic to other areas of life. Am I mocking God and showing my lack of faith by locking my door at night? Am I mocking God by putting a new roof over my house? Should I instead trust him to send the weather that is best to me? Do our fire departments, police departments, and laws mock God? Would we be safer without them? Or do these means assist us in coping with a fallen world?

Christians who support the military do not support it, one would hope, for a great love of bloodshed and violence. They do so, sadly, as an expression of the restraints needed to contain the forces of evil which, unchecked, can create such monstrosi-ties as the concentration camps. The term *just war* is a misnom-er. No war is just, but Christians through the centuries have concluded that the results of fighting some wars are more just than the injustices the war is waged to overcome.

Today the trend is to emphasize the injustices of wars. Author Kurt Vonnegut dwells on the Dresden bombing of World War II rather than the liberation aspects. In the film *Seven Beauties*, Lina Wertmuller states her case superbly. By interspersing scenes from the concentration camps with scenes of American soldiers a-whoring through the streets of Naples, she seems to imply that those Americans who fought Fascism were as bad, really, as the forces they defeated. She seems to say that nothing makes

any difference—Hitler or his demise, the camps or their liberation. Tragedy, comedy, and injustice are found equally in all of
them.

Bruno Bettelheim, a survivor of the camps, wrote a stinging
denunciation of *Seven Beauties* in his lengthy *New Yorker* essay
"Surviving," later published in *Surviving and Other Essays*. He
concluded the piece with this paragraph:

Our experience did not teach us that life is meaningless, that the world
of the living is but a whorehouse, that one ought to live by the body's
crude claims, disregarding the compulsions of culture. It taught us that,
miserable though the world in which we live may be, the difference
between it and the world of the concentration camps is as great as that
between night and day, hell and salvation, death and life. It taught us
that there is meaning to life, difficult though that meaning may be to
fathom—a much deeper meaning than we had thought possible before
we became survivors. And our feeling of guilt for having been so lucky
as to survive the hell of the concentration camp is a most significant
part of this meaning—testimony to a humanity that not even the abom-
ination of the concentration camp can destroy (*Surviving*, pp. 313-4).

Christ came into the Gulag of earth to release the captives and
to bring freedom to the enslaved, and he left us with the charge
to make that our mission. The survivors of the concentration
camps show the worthiness of the project Jesus left with us.
Their morality, art, and sense of hope are glimmers of the immortal soul within them, souls worth freeing and redeeming,
even when it sometimes involves great cost.

A passive watching of the diminution of freedom is far easier
than a committed protest. The lesson of the camps teaches me
that we dare not abrogate our responsibility and pretend that
the lessons from the camps are mere history lessons.

They came printed on direct mail appeals, sometimes indiscreetly staring out from the cover envelopes—the babies with distended stomachs, runny eyes and pencil-thin arms and legs. At first East Asian children filled our mailboxes, then Indochinese, now African. One-third of the world goes to bed hungry each night, we're told, and a cloud of guilt hangs over sensitive Americans.

In 1981, a relief organization invited me to see the relief work in Somalia, which was then being described as a basket-case country comprising the worst human suffering in the world. I expected to return from Somalia with a visceral knot of despair. Instead, I came away encouraged by the commitment and efficiency of relief agencies, yet simultaneously nonplused by the unsolvable problems of development. Because relief work is such a booming business in the evangelical world, it's time we all became more aware of how our money is being used.

CHAPTER TWO

Just This Side of Hell

THE ROAD from Mogadishu to Halba Camp begins as a strip of macadam laid incongruously across the vacant Somalian desert. A flat, sere landscape is interrupted by occasional stands of acacia trees and giant red ant hills that jut abruptly upward like impressionistic sand castles. Few animals cross the road. Giraffes and elephants were killed off long ago. Now only the ugly and the fleet remain: cartoonish warthogs with their sinister tusks and a peculiar style of running with tails held vertically erect, and the diminutive dik-diks, antelope measuring only fourteen inches high.

Along this road ten Marabou storks, four to five feet tall, were standing in a characteristic cross-legged posture. Unlike the beautiful, elegant creatures of legends, the Marabou is more of a vulture poorly disguised as a stork. Its plumage is indeed a lush turquoise, displayed in the stork's odd practice of facing the sun with both wings spread, like a fully-robed pope blessing the masses. But the head attached to that hunchbacked trunk of feathers is all vulture: red, wrinkled, bug-eyed and bald, with a protruding bill designed to rip apart carrion.

These Marabou had gathered around a pool of water with a diameter of maybe twenty feet. We stopped the Land Cruiser and walked toward the water, where the fetid stench of death hung heavy. The evaporating pool contained two kinds of fish: a nondescript silvery variety and shiny black catfish—thousands of fish in all, piled together so densely that the top layer was completely out of the water. Thousands more, dead and dying, lined the muddy sides of the pool. As the land-locked fish near the edges scrabbled desperately back toward the water, the incessant flapping of thousands of fins gave an eerie background accompaniment to the smell and sight of death. The storks stood by quietly, waiting. They had eaten their fill, and would do so for many days until the pool dried up and no fish were left to die.

That water hole was the only one we passed on an eight-hour trip, and I thought of it often as I observed what is happening in the African nation of Somalia. An ancient and handsome people are nearly marooned in a land of vanishing resources. For three straight years in the late Seventies it did not rain in Somalia, and potholes, lakes, and even the two significant rivers dried up. (Somali children count their birthdays only in years when it rains, and today if you ask an eight-year-old girl her age she will likely reply "three.") Water is only one of the endangered resources. Trees are disappearing too, at an alarming rate. The ones that remain are being cut for firewood, and few new trees are growing. They stopped propagating after the elephants were killed off by the ivory hunters. Before then, the elephants would munch vegetation, digest it, and deposit the seeds in moist clumps of fertilizer all over Somalia. No longer.

Somalia can barely feed its people in the best of years. Only fifteen percent of the land is arable, and that consists of a terribly thin layer of topsoil that must be carefully cultivated. But now the scourges of drought, famine, and war have placed the country on the edge of disaster. In the past three years, a million and a half penniless refugees have streamed into the country, many of them a few days away from starvation. No one knows the non-refugee population of Somalia, but estimates range between four and five million. Any nation would find it difficult to absorb a sudden 30 percent irruption of population, but for Somalia it is impossible. Somalia ranks as the fourth or fifth poorest country in the world, depending on the list, with an average annual income of $115.

Somalia now contains the greatest concentration of refugees

in the world, and as a result has become the center of a great flurry of relief activity. The familiar ones are prominent: the Red Cross, the Church World Service, the Swiss government—logos that follow disasters across the globe. The United Nations High Commission on Refugees, recipient of the 1981 Nobel Peace Prize, coordinates the forty refugee camps. But the most visible relief activity involves a new breed of Christian organizations, mostly evangelical: World Vision, the Mennonite Central Committee, World Concern, American Friends' Service Committee, International Christian Aid, MAP International, Seventh-Day Adventist World Service, Food for the Hungry, Tear Fund, the Assemblies of God, and the Southern Baptist Convention.

Muslim Somalia might seem an unlikely place to find such a hum of Christian activity, since estimates of the Somali Christian population range from fourteen to fifty people (precise numbers are difficult to determine since "closet Christians" exist and some avowed Christians are probably secret police). The presence of so many organizations reflects a remarkable development in the giving habits of American Christians. While the media have eagerly chronicled the rise of the Moral Majority and television evangelists in the U.S., few observers have noticed a simultaneous explosion in growth among organizations committed to Christian relief and development work overseas. Two examples: World Vision, based in Monrovia, California, has seen its income zoom from $30 million in 1975 to $150 million in 1982. World Concern, headquartered in Seattle, started with a $67,000 budget in 1975; theirs now exceeds $15 million. It's boom time for relief work, and nonprofit agencies descend on ailing countries such as Somalia with the same enthusiasm that multinational companies show toward economically healthy Third World countries.

The new wave of Christian relief agencies got valuable experience in the refugee camps of Indochina. Fund-raising departments were amazed at how much money flowed in to support their efforts as photos of sad-eyed Vietnamese, Cambodian, and Laotian children filled the pages of news magazines, newspapers, and direct mail appeals, touching the raw nerve of a nation haunted by Vietnam. The horrible drama of the boat people began, and refugee camps were quickly set up in Malaysia, the

Philippines, Singapore, Hong Kong, and Thailand. There, the Christian agencies demonstrated that their personnel had at least as much stamina, motivation, and sensitivity as the old pros at the U.N. and Red Cross. When Somalia slid toward chaos, the United Nations readily agreed to coordinate efforts of the full spectrum of Christian relief agencies.

Initially, Somalia appeared to be a disturbingly familiar mirror image of the Indochina problem: hundreds of thousands of starving and malnourished refugees trudging, homeless, into a country ill-equipped to receive them. But the relief agencies quickly discovered that Somalia, unlike Indochina, lacked the basic infrastructure to support a major refugee operation. In Thailand, if an agency wanted fifty trucks to transport food, a few calls to Bangkok would secure them. In Somalia, fifty trucks were hardly available in the entire country, and there would probably be no gasoline to power them. There were no rice fields nearby, no abundant fruit trees, no roads to many of the refugee camps, no building materials, no warehouses full of medicine. Everything had to be brought in from the outside.

The situation demanded immediate action and the logistics required a massive infusion of outside aid, but one major hurdle remained. The leaders of relief organizations all knew that Americans do not normally contribute to projects in Africa. Some professionals warned of an intrinsic racism that could not be overcome. To complicate matters, the Somalian government followed a rigidly Marxist line of "scientific socialism." How could organizations plunge into one of the most expensive relief projects in history with no guarantee of proper support?

Somalia itself provided the answer, with a spectacular political somersault. For almost a decade after a military coup in 1969, Somalia had operated as a client state of the Soviet Union, welcoming Soviet advisers and giving them vital military bases positioned on the horn of Africa, which guards the oil fields of the Arabian Peninsula. In 1977-1978 Somalia engaged Ethiopia in a vicious war over the Ogaden Desert, homeland of ethnic Somali nomads. In carving up Africa, colonial powers had ceded the Ogaden to Ethiopia, and Somalia was breaking a golden rule of Africa by tampering with existing borders to consolidate its land.

A bloody military coup in Ethiopia, however, ushered in a heavy Soviet presence in that country also, and soon the Soviet Union found itself in the untenable position of propping up two antagonists. Moscow chose to back the larger and more populous country of Ethiopia, and Somalia promptly expelled Soviets from its soil. As Cuban troops and Soviet MiGs mopped up pockets of resistance in the Ogaden, Somalia resigned itself to a guerrilla war and performed a diplomatic about-face. It offered the United States access to military bases that had been built to Soviet specifications in return for $42 million in military aid. Somalia also became the only member of the Arab League to defend Egypt and support the Camp David peace treaty. Fundraising for Somalia was given an obvious boost by its sudden emergence as "our strategic ally on the vital Horn of Africa." Money for relief work poured in.

The sudden plunge into relief work in countries like Somalia has altered the nature of Christian mission overseas. World Vision, the largest evangelical relief agency, had intended to include proclamation of the Christian message as a major thrust in all its programs. But recent political events forced directors to amend that policy. In 1975, for example, World Vision built a seventy-five-bed children's hospital in Cambodia, fully equipped with state-of-the-art medical technology. Days before its scheduled opening, the Cambodian government was overthrown, and Phnom Penh became a deserted wasteland. Eventually, of course, Pol Pot's government also fell after an unprecedented reign of terror. And, while most of the world community, including the United States, was harshly condemning Vietnam for its occupation of Cambodia (now Kampuchea), in 1979 World Vision negotiated an agreement to return to Phnom Penh. It took an additional $1.1 million to finally open the hospital. In order to work in such countries as Kampuchea, World Vision had to agree not to attempt any proselytism or promulgation of the Christian faith.

Each of the Christian agencies in Somalia must similarly restrict their activities—the Somalian constitution forbids Christian evangelism. Somehow the Somalian government obtained an internal memo of one United States-based relief agency which reported that staff "have had extra time recently to witness for Christ." The organization was very nearly thrown out of the country. Christians sharing food and medicines is one thing; ideas are an entirely different matter.

The leaders of evangelical agencies who agree to such conditions justify it in two ways. Some talk in hushed tones about a grand strategy to "soften up" the Moslem (or Communist) world for future Christian penetration. "After all," the president of one group commented, "nothing has worked for those people in the entire history of missions. At least we are allowed into those countries which are sealed off from traditional missionaries."

Others, however, profess no ulterior motives, viewing their activities as a natural expression of Christian love and mercy. The president of World Concern, Arthur Beals, credits the boom in relief work to a raised consciousness among evangelical Christians. "In the early part of this century, when the fundamentalists split with liberals, they rejected not only liberal theology but also the liberal commitment to social action for the poor and oppressed. Somehow those actions seemed less Christian than direct evangelism. Fortunately, that has changed in recent years. People have come to realize that when Jesus fed the five thousand or healed ten lepers he did not first distribute questionnaires to determine the beliefs of his audience. In fact, seventy-five percent of Jesus' recorded ministry was to meet physical and material needs. Relief work is not a question of being a liberal or conservative, but rather of being faithful to Christ's example."

Beals traces his own enlightenment in the sixties to the influence of his son Mark, who participated in rousing anti-war demonstrations and headed a group called Evangelicals for Social Action. While working as a Baptist pastor in Portland, Beals was also affected by Oregon's Senator Mark Hatfield, who has become something of a guru to the followers of Christian humanism.

World Concern, a mid-sized but rapidly expanding Christian relief agency, was one of those called upon to respond to the refugees' plight in Somalia. In April of 1981 World Concern workers agreed to administer medical aid at one particular camp, Halba 1, just forty miles inside the Ethiopian border. In many ways their experience serves as a microcosm of relief work in Somalia, the type of work that lurches into action whenever a major disaster strikes.

While visiting a project in Kenya in April, 1981, Arthur Beals received an emergency message from his coordinator for Somalia. Come quickly, the message said. Morale is scraping bottom. The staff is on the verge of quitting in despair. Beals flew to Mogadishu and took the road to Halba, some 250 miles long, which is paved only halfway. The remainder follows a back-wrenching, rutted trail through unmarked wilderness. In 1981, in contrast to recent years, the rains came to Somalia and the ruts disappeared. Simply getting to the Halba camp was an arduous ordeal. Beals' trip from Mogadishu took eleven hours, including an unscheduled one-hour stop when the Land Cruiser became trapped in a mud pit. Fortunately, a Somalian bus got stuck also, and Beals mustered forty Somalis to help pull his Land Cruiser from the mud.

At Halba, Beals met with his staff of seven who were at the point of frenzy. They had contracted to administer medical help only; another organization was to handle food distribution. But medical supplies ordered months before had not yet arrived, and no food had reached Halba in five days. Sixty thousand refugees were ready to mutiny. When Beals was shown the site where World Concern staffers hoped to erect a makeshift clinic, an old man rushed up to the group, shaking a stick, and screamed, "We don't need a clinic! We need food. Can't you see our babies are starving?" As if to support his words, several Somali women silently pulled out their breasts to show how flat and milkless they were. Other women begged the Americans to take their children away to another country where they would have a chance to survive.

The seven people from World Concern insisted to Beals that they could not possibly provide medical care for sixty thousand people, seventy percent of whom were suffering from severe malnutrition. At least thirty babies were dying each day in the Halba camp. Cut off from supplies, the relief workers had even less hope for solutions than the refugees themselves.

The rain had brought a plague of flies and mosquitoes. Scores of flies swarmed over every refugee child's face, clogging up nasal passages and crawling across the surfaces of unblinking eyes. Dazed and lethargic, the children did not react. The camp doctor, an American, had to take care when sewing up cuts to assure that no flies were caught under his patients' skin flaps before he pulled them together for the stitches. During the daylight hours, when flies were worst, the relief workers could hardly eat without getting a mouthful of flies. The doctor would hold a peanut butter cracker in one hand, between his shirt and bare skin, then stuff his head inside the shirt for a quick bite.

Medically, Halba Camp was hell on earth. Dysentery, whooping cough, measles, diphtheria, and tuberculosis were breaking out everywhere, their symptoms complicated by the malnutrition. Supplies were hopelessly inadequate.

Beals acted quickly upon returning to Mogadishu. Despite gnawing reservations, he accepted the Somalian government's request that World Concern take over food distribution in addition to medical care, and also supervise Halba 2, the refugee camp directly adjacent to Halba 1. It did not take long to track down the mystery of missing food shipments. In those days, corrupt distributors were siphoning off up to sixty percent of all food supplies. Trucks would pull off Somalian highways and openly sell food intended for refugee camps. After numerous complaints, the United Nations Commission appointed a responsible agency to supervise distribution and restore integrity to that system.

Medical supplies and equipment for workers were harder to come by. The most convenient, quickest source was South Africa, but getting anything from South Africa into another African country was problematic. In view of the desperate conditions, World Concern took the risk and ordered $17,000 in supplies. But the Somalian government refused to allow the shipments in, and $17,000 of life-saving supplies ended up in warehouses in Rome. At great expense Beals had the supplies shipped from Rome to London, where the labels of origination were changed, and then back to Somalia. When the shipment arrived in Mogadishu, however, one-half the boxes still bore a damning "Product of South Africa" stamp. The government confiscated those boxes; the others finally made it to Halba.

Back in the U.S., Beals put together an emergency team of ten medical workers, by seconding some from a Dutch organization and recruiting two American nurses. He instructed all World Concern workers entering Somalia to carry in one thousand pounds of supplies as overweight baggage, at exorbitant prices but assured delivery. Within four weeks a vital supply link from the West to Halba Camp was in place. World Concern headquarters in Seattle packed a forty-foot steel trailer with medicines, food, furniture, a refrigerator and stove and an automobile. Two Toyota Land Cruisers were shipped through the free port of Djibouti.

After just six months of intense effort a remarkable transformation took place at Halba. Today, the refugee camp appears as a series of igloo shapes that hug the horizon and stretch out in hummocky rows for miles in every direction. In Somalia, fortunately, the refugees provide their own housing. Many come with a bundle of sticks lashed to a camel or donkey. Refugees without animals simply wander off until they find enough sticks and brush to make a home. After selecting a site, the refugees bend the sticks toward the center of a circle and fashion a dome by wattling other vines through the supporting sticks. Grass, burlap, plastic, or paper is woven through the sticks, or thrown over the top, as protection from the elements. From the distance, all the clustered huts appear identical, like some Boy Scout Jamboree with standard-issue shelters, but up close they are seen as custom-made. (No one knows exactly how many huts, or refugees, are in any camp; the United Nations is considering designating a census day on which refugees would line up outside their huts and a photographer would fly overhead and make aerial photos to determine density.)

A plume of dust announces a visitor's presence miles in advance. Upon the arrival of any vehicle, scores of children, dressed in rags, fill the dirt paths that wind among the huts. Drivers thread their way carefully through the camp, alert for children who dart out without warning; striking one of them could start a riot. The children clamber around the vehicles, chasing them and giggling loudly. This, says a World Concern worker, is the most noticeable change—six months earlier those malnourished children lived a torpid, almost motionless existence. Now the visible signs of malnutrition have disappeared, and Halba children are as active and exuberant as any on a playground in the United States.

The refugee women stand by their huts to watch the commotion. They have a striking beauty—visitors to Ethiopia and Somalia often remark that women there are the most beautiful in the world. They are tall, often over six feet, and elegantly slim. Years of balancing loads of firewood and buckets of water on their heads have given them perfect posture. A diet of milk and a twig that, when chewed, provides the same benefits as brushing and flossing give them perfect teeth. When Somalis smile, their teeth offer a gleaming contrast to their dark, fine-featured faces. Most refugee women have only one "dress," a brilliantly colored cloth slung over one shoulder and wrapped around the waist. Six months before, they wore colorless rags; the bright cloths indicate a thriving black market in the refugee community, most likely supported by stolen food supplies.

Not much happens in the daily routine of a refugee woman. Gathering firewood and collecting water consume almost all her daylight hours. But every few nights sounds of celebration come from the camp as small clusters of Somalis snake through its labyrinthine paths. Deeply reverbrating drums beat a monotonous rhythm, punctuated by the piercing wail of ululating women (a sound made by trilling the tongue against the roof of the mouth while holding a single high-pitched note). At Halba, such celebrations seldom signify a marriage, because so few men are available to marry. More commonly those sounds mark a circumcision ritual about to be performed on an eight-year-old girl. The camp doctor and nurses frequently treat young girls damaged for life by the effects of an unclean knife which cut off more than the clitoris. To assure purity for the future marriage partner, the women also practice infibulation, in which the vagina is sewn shut with a thorn and thread. Sometimes the thread is pulled so tightly that urination is impeded, and a serious infection results. Relief workers do not even try to interfere with these more gruesome aspects of Somali culture, except by repairing the damage afterwards.

Women and children make up eighty-five percent of Halba.

The scarcity of healthy men is a poignant reminder that Somalia is at war. Some relief workers suspect a high percentage of the men are carrying on a nomadic existence nearby, hiding from the guerrilla recruiters who make unannounced visits and forcibly conscript all males. But some of the men who remain bear unmistakable proof of their involvement in the war. The camp commander, a thin, shifty-eyed soldier in his early twenties, is missing two fingers. Veterans often gather in his tent, fill their metal mugs with Somali tea, and swap war stories. One shows off scars where machine gun bullets hit his thigh, arm, and side. Cuban soldiers gunned down over one hundred people in his village, he says. A hunchbacked old man wearing a turban tells of an atrocity in his village. In it, he lost his two sons, fifteen and seventeen, and therefore his security in old age. "What will happen to me now?" he wonders aloud, his rheumy eyes filling with tears. The other men shake their heads and do not respond.

The war rumbles uncomfortably close to Halba, which lies just forty miles inside the Ethiopian border. Sometimes at night workers at Halba can hear artillery fire. A vital bridge at nearby Lugh links the camp with the rest of Somalia and if that bridge were destroyed, Halba would sit defenseless on the Ethiopian side of the Juba River. Two Russian MiGs made low bombing passes over the bridge last summer, and to everyone's surprise the Somalis scored direct hits on both of them with SAM missiles. One of the MiGs, trailing smoke, banked and headed back toward Ethiopia. The other crash-landed with its Soviet pilot just outside a refugee camp in Lugh. The Soviet pilot held off the curious and hostile refugees with his machine gun for several hours until a helicopter arrived to carry him to safety. But no one worries seriously about the threat of invasion—what would the Cubans or Ethiopians want with a sprawling refugee camp?

In spite of occasional reminders of a lingering war and its recent history of death and despair, Halba Camp today seems peaceful and calm. There are no more children with orange hair and bloated bellies, no more old men with wasted flesh clinging to their bones, no more despairing mothers with empty breasts. The women devotedly care for their children, who play games and chase each other through the winding paths of Halba. Older children receive instruction in the Koran at makeshift schools in the camp. One relief worker confided to me his belief that now one-third of the refugees are not primarily victims of war or famine, but rather local nomads who have settled down to enjoy the free services of the stable camp.

In America and Europe, television reports and relief agencies still depict Somalia as a disaster area with diseases decimating the masses of starving refugees. But those photos and images are mostly dated. They are used because of the sad truth that hope does not raise money. The fact that people are now receiving food and medicine is not a sufficient stimulus for a giving country; crisis appeals to fear and guilt work far better. Therefore, the remarkable improvements made by the relief agencies in Somalia must go largely unreported to donors. Their own success would kill them.

The expatriate staff responsible for such transformations at Halba consists of seven nurses from Holland, a Dutch mechanic nicknamed "Golden Hands," a Finnish midwife and medical director, and twelve Americans (a doctor, four nurses, two community development workers, two cooks, and three support persons). Although living conditions have drastically improved with restored supplies, Halba presents several obstacles to comfort not normally encountered in Finland, Holland and the United States. First, there is the heat. Somalia has two seasons, rainy and dry, better known as the mud season and the dust season. Since Halba is barely a hundred miles from the Equator, both are mercilessly hot: one, a steamy heat, and the other, a searing heat.

The rainy season brings the flies and mosquitoes. Later, as the rains drift out to sea, strong winds, stirring up choking clouds of dust, dry up most breeding grounds and offer respite from those insects. But in the dry season scorpions emerge from hiding, usually on moonless nights. Sometimes at night the relief workers at Halba hear an eerie, howling sound, like that of a wounded wolf, carrying across the thin desert air. The sound gets louder and louder as its source becomes clear: a nomad, stung by a scorpion, has come to the camp for pain medicine.

After a scorpion stung her arm, one Halba nurse was incapacitated for three days and required a Novocain shot every four hours. She described the pain as "childbirth multiplied by twelve." Halba's only doctor, John Wilson from North Carolina, was stung in the face while sleeping one night. A baby scorpion had crawled up the slope of his tent and then dropped onto his face. He awoke in searing pain, fumbled around for his shoes and flashlight and went outside to find the nurse for an injection. Just outside the tent he stepped on a squirming five-foot-long poisonous snake. On the path to the nurse's tent he spotted four more scorpions glowing phosphorescently in the darkness. Halba is a far cry from North Carolina. Dr. Wilson gets revenge by collecting scorpion specimens, preserving them in formaldehyde and mounting them. He is proudest of his collection of camel spiders: huge, hairy creatures larger than a man's hand that can inflict a wound as painful as a scorpion's but with toxic side-effects.

Relief workers must also avoid the dangerous crocodiles lurking in the Juba River. African crocodiles grow as long as eighteen feet and weigh up to two tons, and yet can maneuver with surprising agility on land. One refugee, a pregnant woman, met her death while bathing in the Juba. Onlookers saw the flash of a horny snout, heard a cry of terror, and watched helplessly as a trail of bubbles disappeared downstream.

The relief workers live on a bluff overlooking the Juba, in an area cordoned off by a crude fence of piled-up thorn bushes. Their canvas tents have been so battered by the wind that zippers and mosquito nets no longer function. A small but thriving vegetable garden grows along the bank of the Juba, a project designed to interest the Somalis in agriculture. Camp workers also have a kitchen, well stocked with boxed and canned foods, which includes one refrigerator and two stoves. Two roofless latrines stand some distance away.

Even in remote Somalia, a refugee camp is energy-dependent: kerosene for the lamps, propane for the stove, diesel for the water pump. All food is donated by the West, as are medical supplies. The usual nomad/visitor relationship has been reversed. Under normal conditions, nomads would have the advantage over Westerners of being able to live off the land. Now the war and drought and resultant overcrowding have made refugees totally dependent on the relief workers and their steady stream of supplies—an umbilical cord to the West sustains them. "If our supplies were interrupted for a week or ten days," said the Somali camp commander, "people would begin to die."

The daily routine of relief workers begins early, since clinics and food distribution stations open at seven o'clock. From noon until four in the afternoon everyone in the camp, refugee and relief worker alike, withdraws to shade or indoors to avoid the afternoon sun. Another round of work starts at four and lasts until dinner-time at seven. There are few diversions for the relief workers. Except for reading the few well-thumbed books and magazines at Halba, there is little to do. At night they often gather around a campfire, discuss the day, and reminisce about their respective countries. Most also served in Indochina and reflect nostalgically on those days in a less primitive setting. Once every three months the workers get a week in Mogadishu, and after six months, a partially paid vacation in the Seychelles or Nairobi.

What attracts people to a daily regimen of low-paid work under the equatorial sun with few of the amenities of modern life? Dr. John Wilson, a soft-spoken, silver-haired pediatrician from Black Mountain, North Carolina, mentions a sense of duty. "Sometimes I feel like Jonah out here—I came because I thought I should, whether or not I felt like it. My father was a missionary doctor in Korea, beginning in 1907, the only doctor serving five million people. I have worked in Korea also, among ten thousand leprosy patients after the war. Professionally, I've tried a little of everything—a busy private practice, teaching at a university and working with coal miners. Over the years I've come to believe I ought to tithe not just my money but also my time to God. My wife's health keeps us from living overseas for long periods, so I accept short-term assignments and spend the rest of the year with my practice in North Carolina."

Among other factors, Dr. Wilson refers to the attraction of medical pioneering. "After seeing hundreds of children all year who may have nothing more than a runny nose or a sore throat, it does something to me to come over here and have a part in saving lives." The doctor who preceded Dr. Wilson performed one memorable appendectomy by flashlight inside a tent during a driving rainstorm. He used two tablespoons as retractors and dish towels as sponges. In Somalia, a dental hygienist pulls teeth and performs basic oral surgery. There are no insurance bills to pay, no malpractice suits to worry about. Most relief workers, in fact, are surprised by the resigned fatalism of the Muslim patients, who do not cast blame or complain if a treatment fails. If a baby dies, Allah has willed it.

Dr. Wilson's age is an exception among the relief workers in Somalia. The vast majority are in their early twenties—idealistic, fresh-faced youth who could be posing for a Peace Corps poster. Jeans and T-shirts have become the national uniform of relief work overseas. Lois Kelsey, a twenty-one-year-old blonde who wears her hair in pigtails because Somalis consider it modest, shrugs off the hardships of life in a camp. "How could anyone feel sorry for me?" she says. "Six months ago I was studying nursing in the tree-lined suburb of Oak Park, Illinois. Most of my friends from class are now grinding out the three-to-eleven shift at some hospital. They're the losers. I'm having the adventure of a lifetime—my perspective on the world will never be the same."

Lois grew up in Jordan among Palestinians. "Nomads are wonderful to work with because they are so fiercely independent. They aren't even tempted by a life of material luxuries. They take pride in being able to walk for two days without food and feel no hunger. In Jordan, I saw the tragedy of such people uprooted from their life style and herded into camps. Their families and culture began to disintegrate. I decided back then that I wanted to spend my life trying to interrupt that process of decay in a beautiful culture." At a very early age she took on the goal of working among displaced persons, Muslims and nomads. In Somalia, she has all three. Lois has high praise for two hundred Somali "health auxiliaries" whom she and the other relief workers supervise.

The government of Somalia observed health care in the refugee camps of Thailand, Bangladesh, Malaysia, and the Philippines and concluded they were too dependent on a Western mode of treatment. Therefore it decreed that most of the health work in the camps be carried out by volunteer Somalis trained to treat the most common ailments. Twenty diseases are officially recognized and posted in bold print in all the clinics (a category, number twenty-one, is labeled "other").

Perhaps ten percent of the refugees, mostly late arrivals, are still affected by malnutrition, and their weakened states make them more susceptible to disease. Sixty thousand people living in close quarters, with poor sanitation, and a breeding ground for flies and mosquitoes nearby, combine in what one camp worker calls "a timebomb of communicable disease." Diseases like measles and whooping cough hit the camp in waves, taking the weak. Nearly every refugee in the camp has some latent form of malaria. Expatriate relief workers drill their Somali volunteers in the symptoms and treatment of those top twenty diseases. The health workers get no pay or special treatment and they, too, must roam for water and firewood and care for their families. Yet most take their training so seriously that Lois estimates ninety percent of the health work could continue if all expatriates left. "They're the best thing we have going," she says. "We'll all be gone someday, but they will stay. If we do our training right, they can permanently change the culture for good."

In just six months, relief workers have moved Halba Camp from a flashpoint of disaster into an organized community with basic food and medical needs supplied. Short-term emergency goals have been met. A far greater challenge lies ahead: dealing with the long-term implications of the refugee crisis. Indochinese refugee camps were holding stations where refugees waited until Western host countries could absorb them. In contrast, no one is lobbying to relocate Somali refugees in other countries. And yet few observers there judge the nation of Somalia capable of absorbing them. As long as the war drags on, refugees cannot return to their homelands.

(Some cynics believe the government of Somalia itself is not overly anxious to solve the refugee problem. Relief work is now the leading source of foreign exchange in the country—business has never been so good in downtown Mogadishu. In the summer of 1981 Somalia devalued its currency by fifty percent, which ordinarily would greatly strengthen the dollar there. But the government callously exempted all foreign organizations, so that relief agencies now must effectively pay a one hundred percent markup on Somali goods.)

While Somalia has extended an open hand to scores of relief agencies, which in turn have made giant strides toward stabilizing the refugee problem, every outside interference brings its own long-term consequence. Refugee camps, for example, ruin the grazing capacity of the land. As nomads, Somalis never stayed in one place long enough to cause irreversible damage to vegetation. But drilling a borehole or providing a water supply at a stationary camp allows the livestock and goats to trample the ground until the root systems of vegetation are destroyed. A seeming improvement, a well, actually proves destructive.

The communal search for firewood also denudes the landscape. Halba Camp was first located in the shade of a forest, an unheard-of luxury among Somalia's camps. Each month, however, the number of trees shrinks as refugees ignore rules and tear down remaining trees. Refugees must now walk eight miles for firewood. Soon they will walk ten, then twelve. Goats and donkeys will eat the new green shoots of trees, and in a few years the forest will vanish forever, replaced by the desert. For the people at Halba to survive, massive changes must come. But no one seems very sure what those changes should be.

The camp director has one idea: he is now teaching Halba's children to fish in the Juba, where a fast-growing species called *talapia* abounds. Somalis in the camp have never tasted fish— hundreds starved to death within sight of a river glutted with them. The children are trying the new idea, to the disdain of their parents. Agriculture faces even greater resistance. Before returning to the United States, Dr. Wilson sketched out a crude design for a passive flow irrigation system. The Juba falls sharply near Halba, and a pipe buried in the river upstream could follow a downward slant and provide energy-free water for irrigation. If money can be found, the Halba workers may install such a system. But there is no guarantee that the Somalis will use it. Their abhorrence of the settled agricultural life runs very deep. None of them has shown any interest in the camp garden.

"Water is the best feature of Halba Camp," says Dr. Wilson, "but it is also the biggest health problem. We could probably prevent half the illnesses in this camp if we could just teach the refugees not to drink the river water. We have a German-built filtration system that pumps river water through three treatment tanks. It's not totally pure—if we purify it completely, then the infants will grow accustomed to distilled water and will build up no resistance to the germs they'll find in water when they leave the camp. But the refugees at the extremities face a difficult choice. Should they take our advice and walk three or five miles for filtered water, carrying a heavy load back to their huts? Or should they do as they have always done and scoop it from the river a few hundred yards from their homes? So far, only a few of our Somali health workers have been effective in warning them against drinking the river water."

Relief workers don't talk much about another problem that, to their executive officers back in the United States, looms as the largest long-term problem of all. Will fickle American givers, who underwrite all their salaries and life-giving supplies, grow tired of Somalia? Before long, word will reach contributors in the States that the crisis in Somalia has faded somewhat, and funds will surely drop off. Relief organizations are at the mercy of the cruel realities of fund-raising. They need a crisis atmosphere to sustain interest in Somalia.

Fund-raising techniques vary across continental lines. In Europe, an anti-Communist appeal brings in millions of dollars. Underground Evangelism supports a relief agency in Somalia called International Christian Aid by telling of exploits of smuggling Bibles behind the Iron Curtain. Australia and New Zealand have the most demanding donors, say the experts. They want hard, discriminating facts about specific relief projects. But Americans require emotional heat: tearful white bwanas holding dying infants in their arms and looking pleadingly into the camera lenses. European photographers don't usually perform well for American fund-raisers—their photos are too "pretty" and landscapy, not emotionally gripping enough.

Fund-raising, like any $50 billion industry, operates according to scientifically measured principles. The Preview House in Hollywood can judge the relative appeal of a fund-raising approach. There, 450 carefully selected people sit in chairs and react to visual clips by moving a response dial from "low interest" to "high interest." Computers in adjacent rooms integrate the response data, combine it with demographic information and read out exactly what slant appeals to each category of person. Children are the biggest draw, which is why so many of them stare out from the pages of slick magazines appealing for funds. A bona fide celebrity also helps. Commercials are measured in that room, as are soap opera segments and television quiz shows. And there America's fund-raisers keep confirming the inescapable reality that emotional appeals based on guilt sell, not development projects based on hope and an improved life style.

The executive director of one major relief organization, who asked not to be identified, expressed his dilemma this way. "I tell you, the temptation is very strong for me to start up an 'Adopt a Child' program, whether it is needed or not. Those adoption programs are guaranteed fund-raisers, although they are bureaucratic nightmares. Since the government started scrutinizing them several years ago, some agencies now spend $12 of each $17 they take in on the overhead, just to keep track of the children and communicate the specifics to the donors. I can't justify that.

"We got talked into Guatemala by another relief agency, and I'll always regret it. So much food was dumped down there after the earthquake that it put the local entrepeneurs out of business. I have vowed to stop ambulance-chasing. I won't go into a country that suddenly appears in news headlines just to clean up on the fund-raising dollars that are sure to follow. But to do any kind of meaningful development, I must feature the crisis aspects of a place like Somalia. I admit it, our film footage is six months old. But people will give money on that emotional appeal. About half the donors will specify their gift for emergency food or medicine supplies. The other half will check 'Use as needed,' and that's all the money I have to work with for true development activities."

The field of health services provides the most striking example of the conundrum of relief work. People will eagerly donate drugs and medical supplies to combat outbreaks of diseases. Mission hospitals readily attract donors. And yet, as wise health professionals know, those responses to health problems do not attack the underlying causes of disease. Civilized countries experienced steep declines in the incidences of bronchitis, pneumonia, influenza, tuberculosis, whooping cough, measles, and scarlet fever long *before* any effective immunization or therapy became available. Improved nutrition and sanitation did far more to disarm those diseases than any treatment devised by medical science. Parisian sewers were more effective than a hundred hospitals. The World Health Organization estimates that eighty percent of all health problems in the Third World relate to polluted water supplies. But try to raise money to clean up a river, or install a passive irrigation system, and you won't cover the cost of the mailing.

'A million people are plunging like lemmings off a cliff," muses one relief worker. "We can easily raise money to pick up the survivors and nurse them back to health. But there are no funds at all to set up prevention and warning programs at the top of the cliff."

For the present, it seems, relief agencies need situations like Somalia as bad as Somalia needs relief help. The experience of that country summarizes everything right and wrong with relief work. For the short term, relief agencies have worked miracles. Masses of people have been kept alive, fed and medically treated in an extraordinarily brief period of time. The logistics of a poor country with no infrastructure absorbing a thirty percent increase in population have somehow been overcome. For the moment, the crisis in Somalia is no longer a life-or-death matter, as long as the tenuous thread of help from the West stays intact.

No one knows, though, what might happen in the long term as the focus changes from relief work to development. Money itself is no guarantee of success in development. Africa's greatest previous crisis was a devastating drought in the Sahel Desert that killed up to one hundred thousand people and twenty million cattle. In the past ten years a consortium of European agencies has spent eight billion dollars to "drought-proof the Sahel." Realists admit that the Sahel is no better off now. Mismanagement and ecological complexities have undermined any hope for substantial change. The Sahel continues to encroach on fertile land. Some relief workers predict that in a decade or two there may not be a single surviving tree left in the entire region.

The Somalian government is just beginning to adjust to the fact that the camps—forty cities spread across Somalia—may turn into permanent settlements of squalor, somewhat like the Palestinian camps. Yet the land simply cannot support that kind of concentration; finite water and firewood resources will not allow it. Will the Somali nomads forfeit an entire cultural history and embrace agriculture or industry or fishing? Will the West continue the massive outpouring of aid required to support such a change?

The relief workers in Somalia are just now beginning to consider such questions. Their experience there vividly illustrates a universal principle of relief work: in relief, as in wars, it is far easier to get in than to get out.

My research into Wycliffe began when Reader's Digest asked for a profile on Cameron Townsend, the mission's founder. Trips to Seattle, Los Angeles, and New York City acquainted me with the mission's cumbersome bureaucracy. Mission leaders, though gracious and polite, seemed initially gun-shy of talking to the press. In recent years they have been reeling from a series of controversies, and publicity has not always helped.

In Waxhaw, North Carolina, I met for three days with Uncle Cam, who had just celebrated his eighty-fifth birthday. His long life was a mixture of triumph and sadness: he has been honored by Christian leaders and presidents of nations, and yet what counted most, his singular lifelong goal, proved unattainable.

As Cameron Townsend's mind and body slowed down, the Brobdingnagian organization he founded is lurching into the computer age. Wycliffe, the largest Christian mission, faces pressing, complex issues. Its response to them may well set the pace for the entire modern mission movement.

CHAPTER THREE

A Mission in Search of a Future

CHESTER Bitterman's body was found, blindfolded, propped up on the front seat of a bus, with a single bullet wound through the heart. The revolutionary M-19 movement which had kidnapped him left one last vestige of their presence: a red and black guerrilla army flag enshrouding his body. It was a rainy, oppressive day: March 7, 1981. Word spread quickly through the streets of Bogota, and finally a shopkeeper banged on the gate of Brenda Bitterman's residence and informed her with a shout, "They've found Chet's body in a bus!"

The Christian world, kept anxious and prayerful during the forty-eight suspenseful days of captivity, experienced a numbing sense of *deja vu*. It had happened before, this paroxysm of sadness and shock, the massive world attention focused on missionaries in South America, the word "martyr" slipping into press accounts, the attempted explanations from the pulpit on why God would allow such a young, dedicated servant to be killed. Minds went back twenty-five years to that haunting day in 1956 when a plane, stripped of its skin, was found on Ecuador's Curaray River, and sprawled beside it the murdered bodies of five young missionaries.

That Auca slaughter ultimately proved to be a watershed of modern missions. The missionaries' sacrifice galvanized the Christian community. Hundreds of young people volunteered to replace the missionaries who had fallen. A remarkable sequence of photographs in *Life* magazine elicited more response from readers than any story in the magazine's history. The man who took these photos, a Jewish Hungarian immigrant named Cornell Capa, began a strange friendship with missions that has continued to this day. Eventually, Elisabeth Elliott, wife of one of the martyrs, would emerge as an author to tell the complete story.

Bitterman's death in Colombia evoked a similar response. Newspapers filled their front pages with accounts of his kidnapping and attempts to explain the work of his organization, the Wycliffe Bible Translators. More importantly, at memorial services hundreds of young people volunteered to "go and take Chet's place."

Yet the Auca and the M-19 tragedies are marked by profound differences which signify the epochal changes that have occurred in the last twenty-five years of foreign missions. Upon reflection, the Auca tragedy appears as a simple black-and-white affair. It occurred when America was riding a wave of post-War popularity, before Vietnam and before many of communism's advances. Five clean-cut, smiling, good-natured men descended like gods from advanced civilization into the heart of the land of savages. They were attacked without provocation, killed by Auca spears. In a sense, they symbolized America the virtuous, attempting to bring the best values and the best of civilizations to a world trapped in darkness. No editorials anywhere extolled the cause of the Aucas or questioned the inherent rightness of the five missionaries' goals.

Chet Bitterman died in a world vastly changed. Everything is messier now, less clear-cut. The press in Latin America devoted as much space to complaints about Wycliffe as to the details of the guerrillas' crime. Bitterman too was seen as an agent of America, but this time it was a damning charge: *Did he work with the CIA?* headlines asked. References to liberation theologians, revolutionaries, and embittered anthropologists mingled in press reports with explanations of Wycliffe's mission.

The world has changed, and no Christian organization feels it more acutely than Wycliffe Bible Translators, a movement that has achieved phenomenal success in less than fifty years of existence. Tremors, signs of warning, have been building in intensity for the past decade. Partly because of its success and resultant visibility, and partly because of its unique *modus operandi*, Wycliffe will be near the epicenter of change for the next few years. Other mission agencies will watch the impact on Wycliffe and adapt accordingly.

Controversy is hardly new to Wycliffe; the organization has endured a series of mind-boggling accusations over the years. Rumormongers in Peru in the 1950s accused Wycliffe of boiling Indian babies to produce jet fuel. In 1972, Colombian authorities took other rumors so seriously that a unit of the Colombian army descended upon Wycliffe's main center, Loma Linda. A three-day search of a lake by frogmen failed to turn up any sign of the suspected underwater missile base and uranium mine, and Wycliffe was allowed to continue operations.

Wycliffe has also faced bitter criticism from within evangelical ranks. In the 1950s some of the grumblings centered on Wycliffe's practice of transporting nuns and priests in its airplanes. Other missionaries decried such acts of kindness toward a Catholic church which, in those pre-Vatican II days, often opposed evangelical work. Cameron Townsend, Wycliffe's founder and president, would not budge despite withering attacks. "How can I let a sick nun languish in a jungle outpost when we have the capacity, with our airplanes, to bring her to a hospital?" he asked. "Aren't we there to serve?" In fact, he went out of his way to cultivate friendships with Catholics, preparing packages of cookies and newspapers for his jungle pilots to drop off at Catholic mission stations. The furor in the United States became so heated, however, that Wycliffe decided to resign from the Interdenominational Foreign Missions Association in 1959. The Christian world has changed in twenty-five years too.

Today the issues facing Wycliffe are more political in tone. Topping the list in Third World countries is the suspicion that Wycliffe cooperates with the CIA. Newspapers in some Latin American countries daily carry major stories accusing Wycliffe of a CIA connection. In the Third World, there is no more damning calumny.

No one has yet been able to produce evidence substantiating

the CIA charge, although journalists have spent months looking for corroborating evidence. Wycliffe officials insist their organization is clean. Most of the charges, they say, originated in the murky swamps of Vietnam. There, after Wycliffe linguists trained Montagnard tribesmen to read and write, CIA agents swiftly brought in their own favorite reading materials: booklets on how to use M-16 rifles and blow up bridges. "How can we be held responsible for *what* they read?" asks one Wycliffe executive. "We are not censors, just linguists and educators. We merely translate the Bible, but we certainly cannot control what else a culture reads."

In training programs, Wycliffe tells its members that any who willingly give information to the CIA will be dismissed. At least five times CIA officials have asked Wycliffe executives for access to information and have been refused. In three countries Wycliffe has been the channel for AID funds earmarked for schools and supplies, and the United States has admitted some CIA influence on the use of other AID funds, but other than that very tenuous link, no questionable practices have surfaced.

Why, then, do charges linking Wycliffe and the CIA proliferate? Third World critics of all persuasions know well that a CIA stigma would permanently stain the reputation of Wycliffe and hamper its effectiveness in their countries. Repetition of the charge thus creates an underlying suspicion about the organization and keeps governments friendly to Wycliffe on the defensive. In addition, Wycliffe's efficient fleet of fifty-five planes and twelve helicopters and its network of radios linking jungle outposts raise questions. *What are they up to out there?* people wonder. *Are they really devoting all that time, energy, and money to the simple goal of translating the Bible? Surely something else is going on.*

Besides the CIA charge, Bitterman's kidnappers took up the ubiquitous rallying cry of anthropologists: Christian missions are destroying indigenous cultures. Mission leaders bristle at this criticism and counter it with numerous stories of how modern missions have helped, not harmed, indigenous cultures. Yet most mission leaders will freely admit many mistakes of the past, especially when, under the influence of colonialism, missions were extremely insensitive to existing cultures.

To understand the Third World's perspective, imagine a

church in Senegal sending missionaries to the comfortable suburb of Pasadena, California. What if they erected mud huts on the outskirts of the town, reverted to loin cloths and bare breasts and built a thatched-roof church where services would feature their native language and drum-based music? How would the city fathers of Pasadena, or the local churches there, respond? Hymns, architectural styles, and church polity in Third World countries are reminders of former insensitivity to existing cultures.

To be sure, missionaries are not the only culprits. Modern technological civilization rumbles like a steamroller through world cultures with or without missionaries. Ethnic minorities in Russia, China and Arabia have hardly fared better.

In fact, Wycliffe should offer a less inviting target on this issue than other missions. They endeavor to preserve native languages, which act almost assures a culture will persist in some form, despite the inroads of civilization. Still, subtle influences of Western dress, life style, and patterns of thinking leak out and affect the tribes Wycliffe works with. Education opens the door to other, more sinister forces: land speculators, businessmen, oil explorers. Anthropologists point with despair to the Aucas, who, because of world attention, have been severely disrupted by modern civilization. Now Dayuma's son Sammy, educated in the United States, runs a tourist business based in Quito. He flies the curious into the jungle for a firsthand look at the Aucas.

Criticism from anthropologists will only increase in coming years as the number of isolated tribes available to study continues to shrink. Many anthropologists, as cultural relativists, heatedly oppose the introduction of Christian values into cultures. Loud complaints will come from such organizations as London-based Survival International, which espouses the preservation of indigenous cultures. Survival's United States branch is headed by Jane Safer, wife of newsman Morley Safer.

Anthropologists do not normally single out Wycliffe for criticism; they strike out against the entire missionary movement. In the realm of politics, however, Wycliffe stands alone among missions. To understand the reasons, it is necessary to trace some of the chief distinctives of Wycliffe, as developed by its founder Cameron Townsend. Surely one of the most successful and innovative mission leaders, Townsend died in April of 1982 at the age of eighty-five. His career in missions began in 1917 when he went to Guatemala under the Central American Mission as a Bible salesman.

Associates talk of Townsend's singlemindedness: he clung doggedly to a handful of principles throughout his long career. One, of course, was his insistence on the need for Bible translation. He learned that lesson when he realized 60 percent of Guatemala's Indian population could not speak Spanish. "What am I doing selling Spanish Bibles to people who cannot understand them?" he asked himself. So, with no linguistic training and not even a college degree, he settled down in a small Cakchiquel Indian village and promptly translated the New Testament. His translation, with no modern tools, took only eleven years of work, whereas it takes two well-trained linguists an average of fifteen years to accomplish the same task today. (Linguist Kenneth Pike likens Townsend's translation effort to "learning brain surgery with no formal training.") In his spare time Townsend supervised twenty Indian preachers and founded five schools, a clinic, a printing press, an orphanage and a coffee cooperative.

His flurry of activity taught him another lesson, though negatively: do one thing, and do it well. It may be possible to master one language with all those ancillary projects going on, but what about five hundred or a thousand languages? As Townsend learned more about the immense need for Bible translation, he founded a school, the Summer Institute of Linguistics, where he stressed the need to concentrate on the singular goal of translation.

Townsend indelibly learned one more lesson in his early days in Guatemala: cooperate with the local authorities. Being a pragmatic sort, he arrived at that principle while being dragged before the mayor of a town for distributing Bibles without permission. Townsend apologized profusely, and tucked away in his mind a principle he has never forgotten. "Missionaries are guests," he says, "and the government is the host. We must treat them like hosts by getting advance permission for the work which we do."

While other missions were striving for a low profile—especially in Latin America, where the government and Catholic church were so closely intertwined—Wycliffe boldly came out of the closet. Townsend spent long hours sitting outside government offices, waiting for appointments and planning official ceremonies to involve local officials. When the Cakchiquel New Testament was finally published, the first copy went to the President of Guatemala.

"We are here to serve the government," Townsend concluded. "They are our best ally in the goal of linguistics and literacy." Wycliffe is unique among modern missions in this respect. It reports to the government, not to the national church. In most cases, a contract with the government defines their work in a country.

Townsend's innovation, which contradicted everything anyone knew about mission strategy to that point, seemed prophetic from the start. After Guatemala, Townsend approached Mexico, hardly a likely frontier for foreign missions in the early 1930s. A revolutionary-minded government was busily shuttering churches, banning the import of Bibles, and generally causing havoc in religious circles. In his disarming, persistent manner, Townsend plugged away at the authorities, trying to convince them of the need to help their indigenous Indian peoples. Before long, he had a contract with the Mexican government and, amazingly, Wycliffe members were partially paid by the government. For decades Wycliffe members enjoyed special favors not granted to other missionaries: instead of having to truck to the border every six months to renew a visa, for example, they gained permanent residency status.

Townsend perfected his governmental relations technique with Mexico's President Lázaro Cárdenas. His second marriage occurred in Cárdenas' house, with Cárdenas serving as best man. Townsend wrote a biography of Cárdenas, and argued his bitterly contested case for expropriation of American oil companies before the most hostile audience imaginable, the United States Senate. For his part, Cárdenas granted Wycliffe land and buildings, and even donated an airplane for the fledgling work in Peru.

The pattern continued in Peru, Ecuador, the Philippines, and Colombia. Other non-Wycliffe missionaries, accustomed to being reviled in the local press, were astonished to see pictures of Townsend popping up all over: standing in front of airplanes with Air Force generals, dedicating a new school, opening a mission base, receiving awards from national presidents. Obviously, mild-mannered Uncle Cam was on to something.

It took a few decades for other missionaries to adjust to Wycliffe's distinctives. Tinges of jealousy appeared as they watched Wycliffe's cozy relationship with governments earn such lagniappes as hassle-free visas, suspended import taxes, cheaper fuel. Then, of course, there was the problem with the Catholics. Dropping off cookies to nuns and priests? Who were they serving down there anyway? On that point, Wycliffe was unequivocal: *We're here*, they said, *to serve everyone who can help us with our goal of translation.* It was radical missiology at its best.

Some Wycliffe workers even started feeling uncomfortable with the word "missionary." "We're really linguists," said Townsend. "When an ordained minister joins us, we effectively defrock him. We ask him not to marry or bury people. In fact, I discourage Wycliffe members from speaking in churches on the field. Universities, yes, but not churches. It's too easy to get caught up in other Christian work and lose our identity as translators of the Bible."

From its earliest days, Wycliffe was not one organization, but two. In the United States, members are known as Wycliffe Bible Translators. Overseas, and in academic communities, many have never heard of "Wycliffe"; there, the group is known as the Summer Institute of Linguistics. Wycliffe personnel are members of both organizations, and the two have identical boards. National governments find it easier to work with the nonreligious-sounding SIL; American supporters find it easier to support the religious-sounding WBT.

The WBT/SIL distinction has raised eyebrows overseas, and in Christian circles in the United States. *Are they ashamed of being missionaries?* some wonder. Are they going liberal? Why don't they want countries to know they are Bible translators?

In truth, Wycliffe has insisted on a doctrinally pure membership. Many of its members are trained by the same Bible colleges and seminaries as are those of any other mission. They sign a comprehensive statement of faith and show the same outward signs of evangelical fervor as other missionaries.

The decision to specialize in linguistics grew out of Townsend's commitment to the most expedient way to accomplish his goals. He believed missionary work, as traditionally understood, would result. And his thesis has indeed proved out. After a Wycliffe linguist translates the Bible for a language group, converts result and churches spring up. After decades of discouraging missionary work, a virtual revival broke out among the Navajo Indians when a Bible was finally published in their language. There are no "Wycliffe churches" as such, but hundreds of churches and hundreds of thousands of believers have grown out of Wycliffe's work.

So convinced was Townsend of his calling that Wycliffe worked and still works with any language group, regardless of size. Chet Bitterman, for example, was headed for a tribe with only 125 members. Church growth advocates wince when they hear of intensive resources being poured into dwindling peoples. But Wycliffe executives reply, "No one complains about an American pastor with a congregation of 125. And besides, Jesus taught we should leave the ninety-nine and go to any length to find one lost sheep. Our mission is to the neglected people—the five percent who have no written language."

Except for minor skirmishes, the main arena of conflict today is not in the Christian community. Wycliffe Bible Translators has earned the respect of missions and churches worldwide. Townsend is seen as a brilliant pioneer. Some Bible colleges offer courses on three great mission leaders: William Carey, Hudson Taylor, and Cameron Townsend. People may criticize his methods, but the results speak for themselves.

Rather, criticism over Wycliffe's distinctives comes from the political arena, from groups like the M-19 guerrillas in Colombia. The political world has metamorphosed, and Wycliffe's future hangs in the balance. When Cam Townsend first went to Guatemala, communism was still merely a theory being debated in coffeehouses, the world was divided up in a mosaic pattern among a handful of colonial empires, and hundreds of different tribes and languages thrived, undetected, under jungle canopies. All that has changed.

Wycliffe still has cordial, even enthusiastic, relationships with many governments. Its leaders point to invitations from new countries. And in Colombia, government ties proved crucial in the Bitterman episode. The Colombians honored their contract with Wycliffe, despite intense pressure for them to reconsider.

But in other countries, government ties have sometimes proved to be a liability. For example, when President Carter spanked the regime in Brazil for its human rights violations, Brazil "coincidentally" restricted Wycliffe's work. In Peru, the government yielded to pressure and asked Wycliffe to leave, until a chorus of doctors, lawyers, educators, generals, and politicians rose up in its defense. Ecuador clamped down on Wycliffe activity—Ecuador, home of the Aucas! And, in the ultimate insult, beloved Mexico ended its historic special relationship with Wycliffe and refused to grant any more permanent residencies. Nigeria and Panama asked all Wycliffe workers to leave.

These abrupt turns in Wycliffe's relationship to foreign governments relate not so much to changes in Wycliffe, but rather to massive shifts in the Third World. Nationalism is the most potent force in Third World politics. Nationalistic politicians bristle at the thought of their people needing outside help. Some view Wycliffe's well-run, comfortable centers as pockets of capitalistic influence, and Wycliffe linguists as agents of American imperialism. In addition, governments have the habit of toppling. Who is in today may be out tomorrow. If Wycliffe is closely allied to an existing government, it can easily become a casualty when a successor government ushers in sweeping reforms.

Even within the Christian community Wycliffe attracts criticism for its willingness to work with oppressive regimes. *Sojourners* and *The Other Side* question the advisability of a contractual arrangement with a regime like that of Marcos' in the Philippines. Wycliffe responds: "We are their guests. If we foment unrest, we'll be asked to leave. Then who will help the Indians?"

While Wycliffe slogs through the increasingly turbid political morass, other missions face equally complex issues with the national church. How closely should they be allied? Who should serve whom? Wycliffe makes an end run around those problems by bypassing the national church and pioneering mainly among people who have no church.

Cam Townsend was the first major mission leader to espouse the planned obsolescence of missionaries. He insists that when a linguist's task is finished—meaning a grammar, basic literacy tools and a published New Testament—that linguist should move on. Some Wycliffe members are now tackling their third language. In Bolivia, Wycliffe is preparing to pull out voluntarily since all its work there is drawing to completion. Wycliffe plans a ceremony, hoping that the attention will help convince doubters that they have no ulterior motives or desire to stay after their goals are completed.

Obviously, Wycliffe has done something right. The problems it faces now are outgrowths of its success and visibility. In less than fifty years it has grown from one employee to 4,255 making it the largest Christian mission in history. At the beginning of the twentieth century the Bible had been translated into sixty-seven languages. Now portions of it exist in seventeen hundred languages, translation work progresses in twelve hundred more, and work begins in a new language every thirteen days. Much of this energy has spun out centrifugally from the vision of Cameron Townsend.

Unlike some missions, Wycliffe has the luxury of easily understood, quantifiable goals. Other missions espouse such goals as "evangelizing the world," but centuries of effort have produced little effect in places such as Japan and the Moslem world. In contrast, one can tally the number of languages in the world and graph out exactly what is needed to reduce all of them to writing.

For Wycliffe, one language requires about fifteen years of work by at least two people, and a $200,000 investment. To accomplish its goal, Wycliffe has gathered together an impressive array of computers, airplanes, jungle bases, Ph.D.s and other resources. Over four thousand scientific publications have come out of SIL, and Wycliffe is viewed academically as a major force in the field of linguistics. Eighteen thousand people have attended SIL training programs.

And yet, huge obstacles remain. How can Wycliffe linguists

ever reach language groups sealed off in such places as Russia and Albania? Cam Townsend took on the Russian problem personally, and made eleven trips to the USSR between 1968 and 1982. Somehow he talked the distinguished (and officially atheistic) Academy of Sciences into translating the book of *I John* into five Bible-less languages.

Political pressures and the heated issues that swirled around the Bitterman case will only increase. Will Townsend's bold principles, devised early in this century, hold up in the tumultuous 1980s? Members of Wycliffe disagree on the answer. Some feel the organization will function best when it scrupulously follows the pattern Townsend set; others argue for a more flexible approach, with less visibility in the Third World.

By far the largest obstacle facing the organization, however, is the sheer vastness of the translation task. In 1955 Townsend was shocked speechless when informed the total languages in the world exceeded two thousand, not one thousand as he had thought. He gulped hard, prayed harder, and adopted a new slogan, "two thousand tribes to go." But even then he had underestimated Babel. The optimistic slogan, "Every tribe by '85" was quietly scrapped as reports of more languages rolled in by the score. Today Wycliffe can vouch for the existence of 5,171 separate language groups, and the total increases each year. Despite all that has been accomplished, over half the languages of the world have no portion of Scripture.

Today, Wycliffe stands on the edge of a clouded horizon. The external stresses it faces have never been more severe. Morale within the organization had slumped in recent years. The number of new recruits sagged badly for a while, and it did not help to have to abandon projects in at least seven countries. But now, the Bitterman tragedy has refocused commitment within the organization. Everyone seems aware that the task will grow even more difficult. An old hymn, a favorite of Cam Townsend's, is heard more often these days.

> Faith, mighty faith the promise sees,
> And looks to God alone.
> Laughs at impossibilities
> And shouts, "It shall be done!"

In 1981 Wycliffe held a Golden Jubilee celebration honoring the fiftieth anniversary of Uncle Cam's Cakchiquel New Testament. At that celebration, Billy Graham offered this encomium: "As I look back over the last fifty years, great events stand out—world wars, the Great Depression, natural disasters. But if I could read God's record of those same fifty years, I have no doubt that one of the most significant events would be the explosion of Bible translation.

"We are in a new era now. But as I watched the space shuttle *Columbia* return from its maiden voyage, I said to myself, 'If we ever make contact with other planets, Uncle Cam will be there translating!' "

I am sitting in an airplane returning from a trip to the Pacific Northwest. In four days, I interviewed three people. One woman was in an auto accident. As she was driving across a desert with her best friend, a drunken driver missed a stop sign and rammed her car. Her friend and the drunk died instantly; the woman survived with a shattered jaw, broken arm, collapsed lung, lacerated face, and various internal injuries. She has recovered now, except for haunting memories and the prospect of plastic surgery.

A young man had a story with a happier ending. He and his fiancee were hiking in a ravine of the Cascade Mountains when an ice bridge collapsed, burying them under tons of ice. The boy chipped his way out with a rock and went for rescuers. A helicopter lifted the girl out and, after spending five months in body cast, she healed perfectly.

The third victim was an eighteen-year-old athlete from Anchorage, Alaska. In high school he lettered in football, basketball, and baseball. But during his junior year he noticed a bothersome lump above his ankle and had it diagnosed: cancer. He lost his leg below the knee.

In the past decade I've interviewed scores of people like these who have undergone extreme pain: a grandmother in a nursing home with two weeks to live; a race car driver in a burn ward. Every time I return from such a trip, I mull over their stories and their responses to pain. I can often read their reaction with one look into their piercing, sunken eyes. Each victim plods through similar stages: questioning, anger, self-pity, adjustment, gratitude, hope, more anger. Some wear this pain like a badge of courage. Others spend years wrestling with God.

Encounters like these led me on a personal quest into the problem of pain that culminated in the book Where Is God When It Hurts? I readily confess that in that book I did not present a neatly packaged solution. I cannot say to each sufferer, "Praise God anyhow!" or "Pray for healing and it will come." And yet scores of letters from readers have convinced me of the need to face the problem of pain honestly and without flinching. "How can a good God permit a suffering world?" is the perennial question rustling through the pages of theology.

CHAPTER FOUR

In Defense of Pain

THE WELL-KNOWN German pastor and theologian Helmut Thielicke was once asked what was the greatest problem he had observed in the United States. He replied, "They have an inadequate view of suffering."

Ask any group of college students what they have against Christianity, and they'll likely echo variations on the theme of suffering: "I can't believe in a God who would allow Auschwitz and Vietnam"; "My teenage sister died of leukemia despite all the Christians' prayers"; "One-third of the world went to bed hungry last night—how does that fit in with your Christianity?"

The problem of pain keeps popping up. Like Hercules' battle against the hydra, all our attempts to chop down arguments are met with writhing new examples of suffering. And the Christian's defense usually sounds like an apology (not in the classic theological sense of a well-reasoned defense, but in the red-faced, foot-shuffling, lowered-head sense of embarrassment).

I have never read a poem extolling the virtues of pain, nor seen a statue erected in its honor, nor heard a hymn dedicated to it. Pain is usually defined as "unpleasantness." Christians don't really know how to interpret pain. If you pinned them against the wall, or in a dark, secret moment, many Christians would probably concede that pain was God's mistake. He really should have worked harder and invented a better way of alerting us to the world's dangers. I am convinced that pain gets a bad press. Perhaps we *should* see statues, hymns, and poems to pain. Up close, under a microscope, the pain network is seen in an entirely different dimension.

In our embarrassment over the problem of pain, we seem to have forgotten a central fact which has been repeatedly brought to my attention by Dr. Paul Brand, a missionary surgeon who heads the rehabilitation branch of America's only leprosarium. "If I had one gift which I could give to people with leprosy, it would be the gift of pain," Dr. Brand says.

The gift of pain. An alien, paradoxical concept. One that might never have occurred to us, but, as we shall see, one that flows naturally from the experience of a surgeon who treats leprosy victims.

Seen from this viewpoint, pain, like man and nature, is an essentially good creation which has been bent in the Fall. It fits neatly into the cosmic Christian scheme.

Consider earth, which brightly mirrors the handiwork of God: brilliant hues and delicate shadings of a sunset or a rainbow; the roiling foam and spray of a dependable ocean tide; the magnificent abstract designs on butterflies—ten thousand wild variations, all compressed into tiny swatches of flying fabric. Yet the sun which lavishes the sky with color can bake African soil into dry, cracked glaze which may doom millions of people. The pounding, steady rhythm of a surf can, when fomented by a storm, roll in as a twenty-foot wall of death, obliterating towns, villages, even countries. And the harmless swatches of color which spend their lifetimes fluttering among flowers are snatched and destroyed in the daily, bloody ferocity of nature's life cycles. The world, though God's showplace, is also a rebel fortress. It is a good thing, bent.

Consider man: the country which produced Bach, Beethoven, Luther, Goethe, and Brahms also gave us Hitler, Eichmann, Goering. The country which fathered the Constitution of the United States brought us Watergate. In all of us, streaks of brilliance, creativity, talent, and compassion jostle with deceit, selfishness, and cruelty.

And so it is with pain. The nervous system which carries it makes possible man's noblest works. Have you ever watched a concert violinist? Each time his finger lowers on a string he has controlled the synchronized movement of a dozen muscles, supported by the balanced tension of scores of others. His fingers fly through the twelve positions, now falling with power and surety, now searching delicately for a harmonic on the E-string, now plucking a loud pizzicato. The nervous system, with its intricate variations of pressure sensations, makes possible his performance.

Of course, you might say, the nervous system has good built within it. But what about when the circuits are shorted out, when a piercing shot of pain races to the brain, drowning the meek sounds of all other sensations? Can that be a gift?

Pain itself, the hurt of pain, is a gift. After years of working with leprosy patients Dr. Paul Brand learned to exult in the sensation of cutting a finger, turning an ankle, stepping into a too-hot bath. "Thank God for pain!" he says.

Doctors once believed the disease of leprosy caused the ulcers on hands and feet and face which eventually led to rotting flesh and the gradual loss of limbs. Mainly through Dr. Brand's research, it has been established that in ninety-nine percent of the cases, leprosy only *numbs* the extremities. The decay of flesh occurs solely because the warning system of pain is absent.

How does the decay happen? Visitors to rural villages in Africa and Asia have sometimes observed a horrible sight: the town leper standing by the heavy iron cooking pot watching the potatoes. As they are done, without flinching he thrusts his arm deep into the scalding water and recovers the cooked potatoes. Dr. Brand found that abusive acts such as this were the chief cause of body deterioration in the leper. The potato-watching leprosy victim had felt no pain, but his skin blistered, his cells were destroyed and laid open to infection. Leprosy had not destroyed the tissue; it had merely removed the warning sensors which alerted him to danger.

On one occasion, as Dr. Brand was still formulating this radical theory, he tried to open the door of a little storeroom, but a rusty padlock would not yield to his pressure on the key. A leprosy patient, an undersized, malnourished ten-year-old, approached him, smiling.

"Let me try, sahib doctor," he offered and reached for the

key. He closed his thumb and forefinger on the key and with a quick jerk of the hand turned it in the lock.

Brand was dumbfounded. How could this weak youngster out-exert him? His eyes caught a telltale clue. Was that a drop of blood on the floor?

Upon examining the boy's fingers, Brand discovered the act of turning the key had slashed the finger open to the bone; skin and fat and joint were all exposed. Yet the boy was completely unaware of it! To him, the sensation of cutting a finger to the bone was no different than picking up a stone or turning a coin in his pocket.

The daily routines of life ground away at these patients' hands and feet, but without a warning system to alert them, they succumbed. If an ankle turned, tearing tendon and muscle, they would adjust and walk crookedly. If a rat chewed off a finger in the night, they would not discover it until the next morning. (In fact, Brand required his departing patients to take a cat home with them to prevent this common occurrence.)

His discovery revolutionized medicine's approach to leprosy. And it starkly illustrates why Paul Brand can say with utter sincerity, "Thank God for pain!" By definition, pain is unpleasant, so unpleasant as to *force* us to withdraw our finger from boiling water, lightning-fast. Yet it is that very quality which saves us from destruction. Unless the warning signal demands response, we might not heed it.

Brand's discovery in the physical realm closely parallels the moral argument for pain offered by C. S. Lewis in *The Problem of Pain*. Just as physical pain is an early warning system to the brain, it is a warning system to the soul. Pain is a megaphone of God which, sometimes murmuring, sometimes shouting, reminds us that something is wrong. It is a "rumor of transcendence," which convinces us the entire human condition is out of whack. We on earth are a rebel fortress, and every sting and every ache remind us.

We could (some people do) believe that the purpose of life here is to be comfortable. Enjoy yourself, build a nice home, engorge good food, have sex, live the good life. That's all there is. But the presence of suffering complicates that philosophy. It's much harder to believe that the world is here for my hedonistic fulfillment when a third of its people go to bed starving each night. It's much harder to believe that the purpose of life is to feel good when I see people smashed on the freeway. If I try to escape the idea and merely enjoy life, suffering is there, haunting me, reminding me of how hollow life would be if this world were all I'd ever know.

Something is wrong with a life of wars and violence and insults. We need help. He who wants to be satisfied with this world, who wants to think the only reason for living is to enjoy a good life, must do so with cotton in his ears; the megaphone of pain is a loud one.

Pain, God's megaphone, can drive me away from him. I can hate God for allowing such misery. Or, on the other hand, it can drive me to him. I can believe him when he says this world is not all there, and take the chance that he is making a perfect place for those who follow him on pain-wracked earth.

If you once doubt the megaphone value of suffering, visit the intensive-care ward of a hospital. It's unlike any other place in the world. All sorts of people will pace the lobby floors: rich and poor, beautiful and plain, black and white, smart and dull, spiritual and atheistic, white-collar and blue-collar. But the intensive-care ward is the one place in the world where none of those divisions makes a speck of difference, for all those people are united by a single awful thread—their love for a dying relative or friend. You don't see sparks of racial tension there. Economic differences, even religious differences fade away. Often they'll be consoling one another or crying quietly. All of them are facing the rock-bottom emotions of life, and many of them call for a pastor or priest or rabbi for the first time ever. Only the megaphone of pain is strong enough to bring these people to their knees and make them reconsider life.

The concept of pain as a gift directly contradicts the common evangelical attitude of avoiding pain at all costs. We seem to reserve our shiniest merit badges for those who have been healed, with the frequent side-effect of causing unhealed ones to feel as though God has passed them by. The church needs to confront pain realistically and affirm that a sick person is not unspiritual. A tornado bearing down on my house will not magically swerve and hop only to the houses of pagans.

Nothing in Scripture hints that we Christians should expect life to be easier, more antiseptic or safer. We need a mature awareness of the contributions of pain, and we need the courage to cling to God, Job-like, despite the world of pain and sometimes because of it. Christianity calls us to complete identification with the world—the *suffering* world—not an insulated scar-free pilgrimage through the world.

There are those for whom pain seems to be in revolt. Bodies wracked with cancer so that nerve cells scream in unison a message to the brain which cannot be heeded. Muscular athletes who suffer a freak accident which bruises the spinal cord and condemns them to a life of paralysis and excruciating misery. To these people, all philosophical explanations and all phrases like "the gift of pain" must sound hollow and sadistic. It is as if they are connected to the pain machine in *1984;* pain has left its natural cycle and becomes a frankenstein.

There are two contributions to the problem of pain that hold true in any circumstance, whether healing or death ensues. The first is the simple fact of Jesus' coming. When God entered humanity, he saw and felt for himself what this world is like. Jesus took on the same kind of body you and I have. His nerve fibers were not bionic—they screamed with pain when they were misused. And, above all, Jesus was surely misused. This fact of history can have a large effect on the fear and helpless despair of sufferers.

The scene of Christ's death, with the sharp spikes and the wrenching thud as the cross was dropped in the ground, has been told so often that we, who shrink from a news story on the death of a race horse or of baby seals, do not flinch at its retelling. It was a bloody death, an execution quite unlike the quick, sterile ones we know today: gas chambers, electric chairs, hangings. This one stretched on for hours in front of a jeering crowd.

Jesus' death is the cornerstone of the Christian faith, the most important fact of his coming. You can't follow Jesus without confronting his death; the Gospels bulge with its details. He laid out a trail of hints and bald predictions about it throughout his ministry, predictions that were only understood after the thing had been done, when to the disciples the dream looked shattered. His life seemed prematurely wasted. His triumphant words from the night before surely must have cruelly haunted his followers as they watched him groan and twitch on the cross.

What possible contribution to the problem of pain could come from a religion based on an event like the crucifixion? Simply, we are not abandoned. The Alaskan boy with an amputated foot, grieving Ugandan Christians, the Toccoa Falls survivors— none has to suffer alone. Because God came and took a place beside us, he fully understands. Dorothy Sayers says:

For whatever reason God chose to make man as he is—limited and suffering and subject to sorrows and death—He had the honesty and courage to take His own medicine. Whatever game He is playing with His creation, He has kept His own rules and played fair. He can exact nothing from man that He has not exacted from Himself. He has Himself gone through the whole of human experience, from the trivial irritations of family life and the cramping restrictions of hard work and lack of money to the worst horrors of pain and humiliation, defeat, despair, and death. When He was a man, He played the man. He was born in poverty and died in disgrace and thought it well worthwhile.

By taking it on himself, Jesus in a sense dignified pain. Of all the kinds of lives he could have lived, he chose a suffering one. Because of Jesus, I can never say about a person, "He must be suffering because of some sin he committed." Jesus, who did not sin, also felt pain. And I cannot say, "Suffering and death must mean God has forsaken us; he's left us alone to self-destruct." Because even though Jesus died, his death became the great victory of history, pulling man and God together. God made a supreme good out of that day. T. S. Eliot wrote in *Four Quartets* (*Collected Poems 1909-1962*, p. 187):

> The wounded surgeon plies the steel
> That questions the distempered part;
> Beneath the bleeding hands we feel
> The sharp compassion of the healer's art
> Resolving the enigma of the fever chart

That uniquely Christian contribution is a memory. But there is another one—a hope. To the person with unrequited suffering, it is the most important contribution of all. Christ did not stay on the cross. After three days in a dark tomb, he was seen alive again. Alive! Could it be? His disciples couldn't believe it at first. But he came to them, letting them feel his new body. Christ brought us the possibility of an afterlife without pain and suffering. All our hurts are temporary.

How to imagine eternity? It's so much larger than our short life here that it's difficult even to visualize. You can go to a ten-foot blackboard and draw a line from one side to another. Then, make a one-inch dot in that line. To a microscopic germ cell, sitting in the midst of that one-inch dot, it would look enormous. The cell could spend its lifetime exploring its length and breadth. But you're a human, and by stepping back to view the whole blackboard you're suddenly struck with how large that ten-foot line is compared to the tiny dot that germ calls home.

Eternity compared to this life is that way. In seventy years we can develop a host of ideas about God and how indifferent he appears to be about suffering. But is it reasonable to judge God and his plan for the universe by the swatch of time we spend on earth? No more reasonable than for that germ cell to judge a whole blackboard by the tiny smudge of chalk where he spends his life. Have we missed the perspective of the timelessness of the universe?

Who would complain if God allowed one hour of suffering in an entire lifetime of comfort? Yet we bitterly complain about a lifetime that includes suffering when that lifetime is a mere hour of eternity.

In the Christian scheme of things, this world and the time spent here are not all there is. Earth is a proving ground, a dot in eternity—but a very important dot, for Jesus said our destiny depends on our obedience here. Next time you want to cry out to God in anguished despair, blaming him for a miserable world, remember: less than one-millionth of the evidence has been presented, and that is being worked out under a rebel flag.

Let me use another analogy to illustrate the effect of this truth. Ironically, the one event that probably causes more emotional suffering than any other—death—is in reality a translation, a time for great joy when Christ's victory will be appropriated to each of us. Describing the effect of his own death, Jesus used the simile of a woman in travail, full of pain and agony until all is replaced by ecstasy.

Your world is dark, safe, secure. You are bathed in warm liquid, cushioned from shock. You do nothing for yourself; you are fed automatically, and a murmuring heartbeat assures you that someone larger than you fills all your needs. Your life consists of simple waiting. You're not sure what to wait for, but any change seems far away and scary. You meet no sharp objects, no pain, no threatening adventures. A fine existence.

One day you feel a tug. The walls are falling in on you. Those soft cushions are now pulsing and beating against you, crushing you downwards. Your body is bent double, your limbs twisted and wrenched. You're falling, upside down. For the first time in your life you feel pain. You're in a sea of rolling matter. There is more pressure, almost too intense to bear. Your head is squeezed flat, and you are pushed harder, harder into a dark tunnel. Oh, the pain. Noise. More pressure.

You're hurting all over. You hear a groaning sound and an awful sudden fear rushes in on you. It is happening—your world is collapsing. You're sure it's the end. You see a piercing, blinding light. Cold, rough hands pull at you. A painful slap. A loud cry.

You have just experienced birth.

Death is like that. On this end of the birth canal, it seems fiercesome, portentous, and full of pain. Death is a scary tunnel and we are being sucked toward it by a powerful force. We're afraid. It's full of pressure, pain, darkness—the unknown. But beyond the darkness and the pain there's a whole new world outside. When we wake up after death in that bright new world, our tears and hurts will be mere memories. And the new world is so much better than this one that we have no categories to understand what it will be like. The best the Bible writers can tell us is that then, instead of the silence of God, we will have the presence of God and see him face to face. At that time we will be given a stone, and upon it will be written a new name, which no one else knows. Our birth into new creatures will be complete (Rev. 2:17).

Do you sometimes think God does not hear? God is not deaf. He is as grieved by the world's trauma as you are. His only son died here. But he has promised to set things right.

Let history finish. Let the orchestra scratch out its last mournful warm-up note of discord before it bursts into the symphony. As Paul said, "In my opinion whatever we may have to go through now is less than nothing compared with the magnificent future God has planned for us. The whole creation is on tiptoe to see the wonderful sight of the sons of God coming into their own. . . .

"It is plain to anyone with eyes to see that at the present time all created life groans in sort of a universal travail. And it is plain, too, that we who have a foretaste of the Spirit are in a state of painful tension, while we wait for that redemption of our bodies which will mean that at last we have realized our full sonship in Him" (Rom. 8:18, 19, 22, 23).

As we look back on the speck of eternity that was the history of this planet, we will be impressed not by its importance, but by its smallness. From the viewpoint of the Andromeda galaxy, the holocaustic destruction of our entire solar system would be barely visible, a match flaring faintly in the distance, then imploding in permanent darkness. Yet for this burnt-out match, God sacrificed himself. Pain can be seen, as Berkouwer puts it, as the great "not yet" of eternity. It reminds us of where we are, and creates in us a thirst for where we will someday be.

PART TWO

Voices

Dr. Paul Brand is known in medical circles for two major accomplishments. First, he pioneered the startling idea that the loss of fingers and toes in leprosy was due entirely to injury and infection and was thus preventable. The theory, radically new when Brand first proposed it as a missionary surgeon in India, has gained worldwide acceptance.

Second, he is hailed as a skilled and inventive hand surgeon, and most major textbooks on hand surgery contain chapters by him. Brand was the first to apply tendon transfer techniques to the specific problems of leprosy patients, whose hands often harden into rigid "claw-hands." (An interview with Brand can be interrupted by long distance phone calls from surgeons who are stumped in the very process of surgery. He shouts complicated directions to them over the phone, and they resume their procedures.) For these accomplishments, Brand has been given the USPHS Gold Medallion Award and the prestigious Albert Lasker Medical Award and has been made a Commander of the Order of the British Empire.

I have spent many days with Dr. Brand in his home at the leprosarium in Carville, Louisiana, and in other cities as well. Our conversations have ranged over many aspects of Christianity—the doctrine of the atonement, the Trinity, evolution, verbal inspiration, social concern—as well as his own avocations of genetics, carpentry, and ecology. He ranks among the handful of brightest minds in evangelicalism and yet, until recently, few evangelicals had ever heard of him. I liked that about him. He had not written a book or started a radio program or named an organization after himself. A promising British surgeon, he had humbly worked among the lowest class of people in the entire world: the leprosy-afflicted "untouchables" of India.

I have spent much of the past five years working on books which have grown out of my relationship with Dr. Brand: Where Is God When It Hurts?, Fearfully and Wonderfully Made, and its sequel. The following interview pulls together snatches of our many conversations.

CHAPTER FIVE

Creation and Restoration: Dr. Paul Brand

Question: You once headed up a research project in which you tried to develop an alternative pain system for people who are insensitive to pain, such as leprosy patients. In a sense, you and your team of scientists and bioengineers were playing creator with the human body. What did this teach you about the creation process God went through?

Answer: Our most overwhelming response, of course, was a profound sense of awe. Our team worked specifically with the pain system of the human hand. What engineering perfection we find there! I could fill a room with volumes of surgical textbooks that describe operations people have devised for the injured hand: different ways to rearrange the tendons, muscles, and joints, ways to replace sections of bones and mechanical joints—thousands of operations. But I don't know of a single operation anyone has devised that has succeeded in improving a normal hand. It's beautiful. All the techniques are to correct the deviants, the one hand in a hundred that is not functioning as God designed. There is no way to improve on the hand he gave us.

I concur with Isaac Newton, who said, "In the absence of any other proof, the thumb alone would convince me of God's existence." I think of the complex mechanical hands you see in nuclear labs for handling radioactive materials. Millions of dollars went into the circuitry and mechanical engineering to develop those hands. Yet, they are so bulky and slow and limited compared to ours.

Question: Nearly everyone would acknowledge the marvelous structure of the human body. But what of the one in a hundred abnormal hands? Why did God's creation include the potential for these exceptions that fill our hospitals?

Answer: A partial answer to that lies, I believe, in the inherent limitations of any medium that obeys physical laws. In his creation of the world, God chose to work with atomic particles that he made to operate according to physical and chemical laws, thus imposing certain limits. Those were the building blocks of creation. At the upper end of the whole process, for his highest creative achievement, God chose to make a human brain that would be independent and have freedom of choice.

C. S. Lewis's example of wood illustrates the limitations of law-abiding material. To support leaves and fruit on a tree, God had to create a substance with properties of hardness and impliability. We use wood for furniture and to build homes because of these qualities. Yet, in a free world, that characteristic invites abuse. Wood can be used as a club to bash someone's head. The nature of the substance allows the possibility of a use other than that for which it was intended.

I am glad that the world is governed by laws: that fire is hot and ice is cold, that wood is hard and cotton is soft. As a doctor and scientist, I must rely on those properties for my techniques of experimentation and surgery. If I could not rely on plaster to be firm, it would be useless as a splint for a broken bone.

At Carville, we eventually had to abandon our own attempts at an alternative pain system partly because of these laws. The substances we tried to use—metal and electronic components—would break down after a few hundred uses, whereas the body requires millions of uses from each of its pain cells. We were unable to come close to duplicating the complexity and flexibility built into the simplest nerve cell.

Question: As you studied the human body, especially in its sensitivity to pain, and as you tried to think like God, did you see anything at all you would have designed differently?

Answer: I would not be so bold as to express it like that, but I have contemplated the choices God must have considered in creating the body. One of the beauties of the pain system in the body is the way in which each pain ending in a tissue fires off its message at a level of stress appropriate to the preservation of that particular tissue. Your foot, for example, reacts dully to pain, since it must be tough enough to face a daily rigor of pounding and stomping. Yet your eye is incredibly sensitive. I visualize the Creator pondering the pain reflex in the cornea. Here is a tissue highly specialized for transparency and thus it must do without a regular blood supply (which would make it opaque). A wound there is a special disaster, and even a small wound could cause blindness. The pain endings are so sensitive that they call for a blink reflex when a thin eyelash touches the surface—no other part of your body would react to the weight of an eyelash.

In setting the levels of sensitivity, the Designer must have recognized that if the eye were made even more sensitive it would be impossible to keep it open in a slightly dusty atmosphere, or in smoke, or perhaps when the wind is blowing. Yet as a doctor concerned primarily with disease and injury, I might have wished for that greater sensitivity.

The same is true with the lining of the trachea and larynx. We get impatient when we are forced to cough, but patients dying of lung cancer must sometimes wish that the Creator had made the mucosa of the trachea less tolerant of tobacco smoke so that their own physiology would prohibit smoking. Even omnipotence cannot please everybody.

Question: Let's talk for a moment about your concept of omnipotence. As I understand it, you view omnipotence in terms of the potential power, not the process it describes. For example, a Russian weightlifter can be called the most powerful man in the world. But his task of lifting the weights he attempts is no easier for him than my lifting to the level of weights that challenges me; he still has to grunt and sweat and exert. Is there an analogy there to the way you interpret God's omnipotence?

Answer: There may be. I don't even like the word omnipotence. The word conveys a simplistic view of the Creator and Sustainer of the Universe, as if he merely had to wave a magic wand and it all came into being. Man's creative effort in producing the Sistine Chapel or the lunar landing craft required tremendous planning and forethought, and I can envision God going through a similar process of planning and experimentation in his act of creation.

The more I delve into the natural laws—the atom, the universe, the solid elements, molecules, the sun, and, even more, the interplay of all the mechanisms required to sustain life—I am astounded. The whole creation could collapse like a deck of cards if just one of those factors was removed. To build a thing like our universe had to require planning and thought, and that, I believe, is the strongest argument for the presence of God in creation.

From the chance collision of molecules you may sometimes derive a sudden, exciting pattern, but it quickly disperses. Some people really think that all the design and precision in nature came by chance, that if millions of molecules bombard each other for long enough, a nerve cell and sensory ending at exactly the right threshold will be bound to result. To those people I merely suggest that they try to make one, as I did, and see what chance is up against.

I see God as a careful, patient designer, and I don't think that the fact that I call him God makes it easy. There are billions of possible ways in which atoms could combine, and he had to discard all but a very few as being inadequate. I don't think I can fully appreciate God unless I use the word *difficult* to describe the creative process.

I like to think of God developing his skills, as it were, by creating amoebae and then ants and cockroaches, developing complexity until he comes to humankind, the zenith of creation. Again, he was confronted with options at every decision. A person who breaks his leg skiing could wish for stronger bones. Perhaps bone could have been made stronger (though scientists have not been able to find a stronger, suitable substance for implanting), but he then would have made the bones thicker and heavier. If they were heavier you probably wouldn't be able to ski, because you would be too bulky and inert.

Take a model of the human skeleton and look at the size of the tiny bones in the fingers and toes. Those bones in the toes support all your weight. If they were larger and thicker, many athletic events would be impossible. If fingers were thicker, so many human activities—such as playing stringed instruments—would be impossible. The Creator had to make those difficult choices between strength and mobility and weight and volume.

Question: And animals were given different qualities based on their needs. Some are stronger and faster than man, and can see and hear better.

Answer: Right, you can only call creation perfect in relation to other options available. Even human types differ. Is an American better than a Vietnamese? The American is bigger, but it takes more food to sustain him. If food becomes short, the Vietnamese will survive because they can get by on a bowl of rice and the Americans will die out. So physical qualities are not good or bad, but good in certain circumstances. I have tremendous admiration for how the world has come out, with evidence of thought behind it. But every stage of development—moving from the inanimate to the animate, single-cell to multi-cell, developing the nervous system—required thought and choice. That's why I define omnipotence the way I do.

Question: When you speak of pain, and even death, you seem to include these within God's overall design for this planet. These are generally seen as evidence of the twisted, or fallen, state of the world. How do you reconcile these elements with your belief in a wise, loving Creator?

Answer: I cannot easily imagine life on this planet without pain and death. Pain is a helpful, essential mechanism for survival. I could walk with you through the corridors of this leprosarium and show you what life is like for people who feel little pain. I see patients who have lost all their toes simply because they wore tight, ill-fitting shoes that caused pressure and cut off circulation. You or I would have stopped wearing those shoes or adjusted our way of walking. But these patients didn't have the luxury of pain to warn them when they were abusing their flesh.

You're familiar with the stereotyped image of leprosy, with its loss of fingers. That abuse comes because the leprosy bacillus destroys pain cells, and the victims are no longer warned when they harm their bodies through normal activity. In this world, given our material environment, I would not for a moment wish for a pain-free life. It would be miserable. I mentioned earlier that ninety-nine of a hundred hands are perfectly normal. The statistics are reversed for those people insensitive to pain: Nineteen of each twenty of them have some sort of malformity or dysfunction, simply because their pain system is not working properly.

As for death, when I look at the world of nature its most impressive feature as a closed system is the lavish expenditure of life at every level. Every time a whale takes a mouthful it swallows a million plankton. Every garden pond is a scene of constant sacrifice of life for the building up of other life. Death is not some evil intruder that has upset beautiful creation; it is woven into the very fabric and essence of the beautiful creation itself. Most of the higher animals are designed so that they depend for their survival on the death of lower levels of life. Having created this food pyramid, and placed man at its apex, the Creator instructed him to enjoy and to use it responsibly. In modern, Western culture, we tend to see a certain ruthlessness and lack of love in nature, but I believe that viewpoint comes from a civilization whose main contact with animal life is through domestic pets and children's anthropomorphic animal stories.

Question: Just a minute, now. It is true that pain and death fit into the present system of life on earth, but weren't these factors introduced as a result of man's rebellion and fall? Are you saying that the Garden of Eden contained pain and death?

Answer: Well, anything I say about the Garden of Eden must be conjecture, because we've been given very little data about it. I feel reasonably sure that Adam felt pain, if his body was like mine. If there were sharp rocks on which he could have hurt himself, I hope he had a pain system to warn him. The pain network is so inextricably woven into bodily functions—it tells you when to go to the bathroom and how close you may stand to the fire, and it carries feelings of pleasure as well as pain—that I could not imagine a worthwhile body in this world without it. Note also that in the curse God told Eve he would *multiply* her pain in childbirth.

And, I believe physical death was present before the fall also. The very nature of the chain of life requires it. You cannot have soil without the death of bacteria; you cannot have thrushes without the death of worms. The shape of a tiger's teeth is wholly inappropriate for eating plant matter (and even vegetarians thrive off the death of plants, part of the created order). A vulture would not survive unless something died. I don't see death as being a bad thing.

Question: But the explicit warning given Adam was, "In that day you shall surely die."

Answer: I think the precise phrasing is important: "in that day." The whole story strongly indicates to me that God was speaking of spiritual life—the breath of God, the image of himself that he reserved exclusively for human beings. I believe Adam was biologically alive before God breathed into him the breath of life; the Hebrew suggests a spiritual life, a direct link of communication and fellowship between God and man. And after Adam's rebellion, immediately, "in that day," the link was broken. God had to search out Adam after his sin. I don't think his curse referred to physical death at all, and I assume Adam would have died biologically if he had not rebelled. As for thorns and thistles and the pain of childbirth, I'm not really adequately prepared to interpret those. We're given so few details of the creation before and after the fall.

Question: It still sounds strange to hear someone vigorously defending pain. You work in a hospital populated by people insensitive to pain. Having met leprosy patients, I can easily agree to the void created in their lives by the absence of pain. But if you worked in a cancer ward, say, among people who feel constant, unrelieved pain, could you praise pain so confidently there?

Answer: I have worked in places of great suffering: the clinics treating victims of the London bombings during the war, surgical wards in Indian hospitals. The one legitimate complaint you can make against pain is that it cannot be switched off. It can rage out of control, as with a terminal cancer patient, even though its warning has been heard and there is no more that can be done to treat the cause of pain. I'm sure that less than one percent of pain is in this category that we might call out of control. Ninety-nine percent of all the pains that people suffer are short-term pains, correctable situations that call for medication, rest, or a change in a person's life style.

In our experiments with alternative pain systems, we learned it was self-defeating to attach a cut-off switch. We had a glove that, when pressed hard, would emit an electric shock. But if the patient was turning a screwdriver too hard and the electric shock went off, he simply overruled the pain signal and switched it off. As a result, he often injured himself. To make a useful system we would have to eliminate the cut-off switch, or place it out of the patient's reach. I can see why God didn't allow a cut-off switch.

Don't forget, absolutely the best pain-relieving drug in the world is the opium seed of the poppy, which people have used throughout recorded history. God did make allowances for pain that rages out of control. There are many ways open to us to relieve pain of a person with terminal cancer.

Question: Have you given any thought to the resurrected world of the afterlife? The Bible gives little evidence about it, and yet you insist so strongly on the necessity of pain in this world . . . what about the next? The Bible hints that in the matter of pain heaven will be radically different.

Answer: I really don't know. Jesus could walk through a solid door in his resurrection body, so it seems clear the afterlife will be governed by a different set of physical laws. There will be some continuity. His body, and those of the three on the Mount of Transfiguration, were recognizable, and it's true that Jesus even bore the scars of his pain from this world. Thomas touched them.

Heaven is a spiritual world, and it's difficult to conjecture what we will be like when our spiritual forms are fully developed. Will children still have resurrection bodies of children? I think of my mother, Granny Brand, who lived to be ninety-five. She struggled as a missionary for seventy years under harsh conditions in India. Gradually the decades of poor sanitation and Indian diseases and poor nutrition caught up with her, and her body was bent and twisted. She thought herself so ugly that she would not allow a mirror in her house. Yet when she rode her donkey into a village, the people who knew her saw her as a beautiful person, a messenger of love. Perhaps we will relate in heaven so much on that basis that physical appearance will become irrelevant. I don't know how pain fits in. If the verse "tears shall be no more" is to be taken literally, then our eyes will be very different, for in this world we quickly go blind without tears.

Question: What about some of the psychological parallels to physical pain? I'm thinking particularly of emotions we generally view as negative, such as guilt and fear. Do you see these as contributing to health in the same way that physical pain does?

Answer: Guilt has spiritual value: it impels you toward cleansing. It is a pain to the conscience that something is wrong that should be dealt with. Two steps are necessary. First, the person must find the cause of the guilt, just as a person must find the cause of his pain. Much of modern counseling deals with this process of rooting out reasons for guilt.

But then a further step must follow: a pathway out of the guilt. Unless it is aimed at cleansing, guilt is a useless encumbrance. Guilt as such doesn't lead you anywhere, just as pain does not: they both simply point out a condition that needs attention. In this sense, guilt is certainly a good thing, if it is directional, pushing you toward something. The *perceived* purpose of it is for you to get rid of the sense of guilt, which you don't like. Underlying that is the more significant purpose of uprooting and dealing with the cause of guilt. It's the same with pain.

In modern society we tend to approach pain as if it were the enemy. We get rid of the pain without asking why the pain came. Pain-killing medicine can quiet the pain, but that can be bad if its cause is not determined. Similarly, I believe modern psychology has concentrated on guilt as an evil and attempted to suppress or excise guilt. Just stop feeling guilty, they say. Live your life as you want. But in the Christian context, guilt is very valuable. It pushes you to right the wrong that is the cause of your guilt and gives you the outlet of forgiveness to purge it.

When used properly, fear, too, is an essential element of human life, a protective instinct without which the human race would never have survived. A mother isn't happy to leave a baby alone until it has grown to have a healthy fear of fire or of heights. Fear also supplies, through adrenalin, increased heart rates and other mechanisms to tap abnormal reserves of strength. The trick is to have the right amount of fear, and to control it properly.

Question: We know that pain and struggle produce character, and that often in the realm of music and art the tensions of childhood result in creative genius. Do you think the tendency in America to try to balance everyone out through self-help books, counseling and advice, and so forth can be unhealthy? I often wonder how a psychiatrist would have handled Beethoven.

Answer: There are problems in this area. One is a trend to eliminate variety. I think variety is exciting and lovely, yet we set up norms and tend to reject people who do not match. If one does not have the proper standard of height, weight, figure, shape of nose, outgoing personality, and extroversion, the psyche is bruised and he or she loses the will to succeed. Anyone who doesn't conform to our artificial goals does badly. When a child is bookish and is clumsy with sports and doesn't shine in conversation, society tends to discard him or her. But that's the material from which research scientists come. I feel we try too much to push people into molds.

Another danger is the tendency of modern culture to remove risk and adventure from life. Most of our excitement happens to us vicariously, as we watch it on television. We shelter our kids, removing them from risky situations, and as a result stunt their growth. I have always maintained that of our six children, I would much rather have four survivors who truly lived, with adventure and self-determination in the face of risk, than end up with six fearful, timid youngsters. Fortunately, all six have survived, but they could all tell you some hair-raising tales of what they went through in finding their own independence.

This tendency to eliminate risk is compounded upon the old. I visited a very tidy hospital for old people, where the superintendent showed me with great pride how each person had a separate room and a clean bed. They lie there all day. I asked why they were not allowed to get up and walk about. He said, "Well, if they do, we find that they sometimes fall and break their hips. If they go outdoors they catch cold and if they meet with each other they exchange infections. By keeping them in their separate little rooms they don't get infected, they don't break their legs, they don't catch cold." I carried away from there a memory of bodies that were alive, but of spirits that were caged.

Question: Your emphasis on restoring the human spirit brings up an interesting line of questions. In rehabilitation, you work with very few patients, lavishing thousands of dollars and man-hours a year on each one. In fact, at Carville the ratio of staff to patients is almost one-to-one, isn't it? Does it bother you that in India millions of people are going without the most primitive kind of medical treatment while these patients receive so much?

Answer: I don't like the juxtaposition of the two cases—people in India and patients here. I work with quadriplegics and other disabled persons who require lavish expenditures of money, yes. The opportunity to work with a person and to help set his spirit free is one of my most inspiring challenges. No effort is too great and no expense should be spared to restore activity to such a one or to help the spirit rise above its physical limitations.

Even in India I was faced with terrible choices of priorities. After I applied hand surgery techniques to the specific case of leprosy, our staff was able to remake hands. We could turn a rigid, frozen claw-hand into a flexible, usable hand and allow a beggar to find work. But our time and resources were limited, so we had to make choices, just as hospitals in the U.S. recently had to make choices among their kidney dialysis patients. Did we give a hospital bed to one long-term case for a year, or to twelve short-term cases for one month each, or fifty cases for one week each? Did we repair an older patient with gross defor-mities or a younger one who had a whole life ahead of him? The most pathetic cases—those with missing limbs and exposed bones—were often the last we would treat; we tried to focus on less advanced cases to prevent further abuse. These were wrenching choices. Yet in no way did that background of alternatives devalue the worth of the human spirits we even-tually treated.

Question: I have heard it said, by an Indian in fact, that West-ern medical advances applied to India upset the natural balance. Years ago, the birth rate was high, but only a third of the babies survived infancy. Now the birth rate remains high, but most of them live. He accused the West, and missionaries in particular, of causing India's overpopulation because of their "charitable" aid.

Answer: And in a real sense he's right. Missionaries on the whole have not been the chief offenders. They're too inefficient and localized. But the World Health Organization comes in with massive resources and wipes out killing diseases. I would have to say I would not go to India with a life-saving mission without tying it to education for limiting population. While in India, my specific task was with crippling diseases; I helped remake human spirits, and that, I think, is wholly legitimate. The expense required by one of our operations could have saved a hundred people from cholera, but I still maintain that spirit-saving activity was worth it.

Question: Jesus said, "Love your neighbor as yourself." Modern media has made that command infinitely more complex and burdensome. Because of television, the whole world is our neighbor. On evening news programs we watch the progress of famines, wars, and epidemics. How can we possibly respond to all of these disasters?

Answer: You can't, not in the sense in which Jesus meant it, at least. You must remember the context in which he was speaking. He meant family, nearby villages, Capernaum. Jesus healed people, but in a very localized area. In his lifetime he did not affect the Celts or the Chinese or the Aztecs. And I think an intolerable burden of guilt such as you describe merely numbs us and keeps us from responding. We must have a sense of touch to those we love.

Westerners, with our opulent life styles, are very sensitive on this point. But I really don't believe that children born in Bangladesh amid poverty suffer all that much more than a spoiled child in a rich country. In Plato's *The Cave*, he pictured people being born and brought up entirely in darkness, and as a result their range of appreciation of beauty, light, and joy was very different from that of a person outside. When they come up to the light, dazzled, they learn to appreciate a new range of happiness. This, to me, is a deep perception of the human spirit. A child develops a norm, above which is happiness and below which is suffering.

Not long ago I was in Bombay, among the awful refugee villages between the airport and the city. Children live in stinking, ghastly shacks, held up by sticks, reeking with human excrement, fleas, and lice. Yet you'll see a child coming out of the hovel and playing tag and hopscotch with a lighthearted air. Their ability to enjoy the basics of life seems greater than that of a spoiled kid the day after Christmas, whining and smashing his new toys out of boredom.

Question: How do you maintain a sense of Christian compassion in your work? In India you saw thousands of patients regularly with the same afflictions. After examining three thousand abused hands, how can you maintain your compassion?

Answer: I don't know that I do it very well. In India I did learn the importance of a sense of touch. Sometimes when we were treating a serious case and had prescribed some drug, the relatives of the patient would go and purchase the medicine, then come back and ask me to give it to the patient "with my good hands." They believed the medicine was more able to help the patient if it was given by the hand of the physician. Interesting, isn't it, that Jesus always touched his patients?

I probably remember a person's hands better than his or her face. I connect a person's occupation with his hands—sometimes I can read it in the hand. I try to individualize what the loss of sensation or the stiffness in his hands means in his work. When I return to India to teach, I can often remember a patient's hands with startling vividness. I'll recognize someone and say right off, "You've lost some more of your ring finger."

Question: Doesn't your emphasis on the personal aspect of mission run counter to some of the trends in missions today, where we isolate which groups are most responsive to the gospel and go after those groups with a specific approach?

Answer: Yes, it does contradict those trends. I don't believe mission work is necessarily more effective as it becomes more specialized. My father moved into a mountain community in India to preach the gospel. Within a year his tasks were part medical, part agricultural, part education, evangelism, and translation. He responded to the needs of the people around him. I think that's Christian mission at its best.

The Christian way of multiplying is the biological way, not the arithmetical way: One becomes two and two becomes four and four becomes eight. I have seen good Christian medical works in India gradually lose their original mission. They become institutionalized, with a building and staff to support, and soon they have to charge fees for their patients. To make the work more self-supporting, they branch out into specialized surgery techniques. Soon they're doing brain surgery with all sorts of sophisticated equipment, and the people they originally came to reach, the poor, malnourished Indians, cannot afford the hospital. Christian witness shines when a young person goes out to work among villagers, working with their sanitation, treating diarrheal disease, improving nutrition, educating on childbirth. Eventually more good is done through this kind of personal ministry, I believe.

Jesus Christ did not have to touch people as he healed them. He could easily, with that same power, have waved a magic wand. In fact, a wand would have reached more people than a touch. He could have divided the crowd into groups: paralyzed people over there, febrile people here, people with leprosy there, and raised his hands to heal each group *en masse*, but he chose not to. No, his mission was to people, individual people who happened to have a disease. They came to him because they had a disease, but he touched them because they were humans and because he loved them. You can't readily demonstrate love to a crowd. Love is generally person to person.

I visited Francis Schaeffer in Rochester, Minnesota, during one of his treatments at the Mayo Clinic. In 1978, while filming Whatever Happened to the Human Race?, *Schaeffer had begun to feel extremely tired and to lose weight. Two days after completing the project he went for a medical checkup which revealed an advanced case of cancer of the lymph. Since then, he has fought a steady battle, relying mainly on chemotherapy, and has managed to stay productive despite the debilitating disease and treatment.*

Unlike many Christian authors, Schaeffer was not "discovered" after death. His popularity billowed in his prime, and he soon fell subject to a blitz of media coverage and critical analysis as well as the normal accouterments of fame. Three film series have featured him, and his books are now available in a set, The Complete Works of Francis A. Schaeffer. *He has lived the last decade under the glare of a spotlight.*

After twenty-two books, what more does Francis Schaeffer have to say? Quite a lot, I discovered. His books typically focus on ideas and reveal little about his personal nature. In three days with Schaeffer, I found him to be remarkably candid in evaluating his own contributions and in addressing issues commonly avoided by most evangelical leaders.

A summary of Schaeffer's life and work precedes the interview.

CHAPTER SIX

The Legacy of Francis Schaeffer

THERE are two kinds of people in the world: those who divide things into two categories and those who don't. Francis Schaeffer has built an impressive assemblage of books, speeches, films, and followers by being one of the best at bisecting the world and slapping on appropriate labels.

What kind of man is Francis Schaeffer? Many who know him only through his writings expect a rigid, rationalistic personality. In fact, he is quite emotional. If you tell him of an acquaintance suffering severely, he may begin to weep, or stop and pray aloud. His wife Edith claims that fame has not affected his sincere interest in people. "If we're in a big hotel," she says, "and we're on our way to a meeting of seven thousand people, he's just as interested in talking and praying with the girl who comes to clean up the room as he ever was. It's not an act. The same day he heard he had cancer, he prayed with two nurses who had come and told him about their lives. I've known him since I was seventeen, almost fifty years, and I can say he hasn't changed. Once when he came for a date, he apologized for being late. He had seen a drunk on the street and had taken him to the Salvation Army for a bed."

In some ways Schaeffer has assumed the role of a modern prophet. His thinning hair is long, his goatee snow white, and he often appears in knickers. He speaks with a sonorous timbre, sweepingly describing the pitfalls of our present day and the decline of Western civilization. Critics assert that, like a prophet, he tends to take himself too seriously. Schaeffer is not given to tentativeness about an issue. Answers come easily and quickly, and are the direct product of his "antithetical" approach. Surrounded by an intensely loyal family and thousands of fans, he can also tend to overestimate the impact of his thoughts. Some who have worked with the Schaeffer family come away grumbling about their "Messiah complex."

But, unlike a prophet, Schaeffer normally lives among a vigorous intellectual community marked by love, forgiveness, and personal concern for the whole man. He is as interested in beauty as in order. And he spends as much time talking about the application of his message in personal, life-changing ways as he does defining the message itself.

Schaeffer's approach should be seen in the context of his own development. He became a Christian as a teen-ager; while reading Ovid he decided he should read the Bible also. As he read, he recalls, "I saw that there were innumerable problems that nobody was giving answers for. But in the Bible I began to find answers. Even though I was finite it put a cable in my hand which bound all the problems together and gave a systematic answer to them."

"In about six months," he says, "I was flattened." He was impressed by the order and consistency of the Christian system as "beautiful beyond words."

After attending Hampden-Sydney College in Virginia, he enrolled in 1935 at Westminster Theological Seminary, which had splintered off from Princeton Theological Seminary in 1929, under the leadership of J. Gresham Machen in the Fundamentalist-Modernist controversy. A year after Schaeffer entered the seminary, Machen was suspended by his denomination for setting up an independent mission board, and he formed the Orthodox Presbyterian Church.

Carl McIntire and some others subsequently withdrew from the new denomination, forming the Bible Presbyterian Church and Faith Theological Seminary. Francis Schaeffer followed the McIntire forces, finishing up at Faith.

Later, of course, McIntire repudiated the direction Schaeffer took with L'Abri. It is important to note that Schaeffer's early training took place amid controversy. Learned men were defining terms, drawing battle lines, splitting doctrinal hairs. Schaeffer survived it all, somehow learning how to listen compassionately to different viewpoints, and to emphasize love and unity in the church.

For ten years Schaeffer was pastor of a church in St. Louis. Then, in 1947, a survey trip to thirteen European countries changed his life. He came away stimulated by the intellectual climate, but deeply concerned about the spiritual state of Europe. Though some countries were experiencing a postwar resurgence in religious interest, Schaeffer concluded that the neo-orthodox roots of their message would doom the long-term impact of the renewal.

For the next five years, Schaeffer was an itinerant evangelist across the Continent and in Scandinavia. He lectured on church history, tracing Christian origins back to the first church in Acts and through the Reformation. He especially attacked the liberal trends personified by Karl Barth whose thoughts he labeled in a 1951 pamphlet as "insanity." Besides lecturing, he and Edith helped churches organize children's work.

L'Abri grew out of the Schaeffers' ministry in the Swiss town of Champery, where they summered. He held services in an unused chapel of the mostly Catholic town. Some girls at a cosmopolitan finishing school began to attend the church, then to frequent the Schaeffers' house. As he recalls, "I was amazed in those discussions to find that I could answer those girls' questions in a way that a lot of them actually became interested."

In 1955 Schaeffer formed L'Abri (French for "shelter") as an independent mission. Response in the United States was mixed: "You mean you're going to open your home to dropout sons and daughters of rich parents, without charging? What will you do all day? What is your ministry?" Edith's book *L'Abri* chronicles the turmoil of those first few years. Their son Franky contracted polio, a daughter battled rheumatic fever, and the whole family had a bout with food poisoning. Worse, their entire village was almost swept away by avalanches, and at one point the Schaeffers were ordered to leave Switzerland for "having a reli-

gious influence on the town." Financial needs were also pressing. They had begun L'Abri with a vow that they would never
directly solicit funds or students.

Word soon got out, among European students and American
visitors, that "There's a man up there in the mountains who can
answer your questions." The trickle of guests began.

Today the Swiss branch of L'Abri services some 110 people at
a time. In addition, many people rent chalets and share in
L'Abri activities. Smaller branches exist in France, England, Holland, and Rochester, Minnesota.

L'Abri is a commendable example of the outworking of practical apologetics (although recent visitors there say the unity of
the place is sorely suffering from Schaeffer's absence). Even
critics of Schaeffer's philosophical approach admit this. Professor Jack Rogers, after analyzing Schaeffer in a two-part article in
The Reformed Journal concluded, "In reading their (Schaeffers')
books I have found the inexactitude of the arguments exasperat-
ing, but the description of life at L'Abri exhilarating."

While L'Abri can affect only a few score people at a time,
through books and films Francis Schaeffer's thoughts have
spread throughout the world so that today he is hailed as one of
evangelicalism's leading spokesmen. "Missionary to the intellectuals," *Time* called him. And *Eternity* said he has "more influence with today's youth—from members of the dropout world
to the disillusioned heirs of evangelicalism—than any other
man."

Schaeffer's twenty-two books have sold well over three million copies, not to mention his wife's books and those of other
L'Abri staff members. InterVarsity Press even markets a booklet
called "Introduction to Francis Schaeffer" in which he explains
how all the various books fit together. The books tend to be
repetitious and didactic, but they cover a broad range of topics,
and all are readable by the educated consumer.

His first book came about after Schaeffer had been touring
colleges and universities in the United States delivering a lecture
called "Speaking Historic Christianity Into the Twentieth Century." He got an enthusiastic response at Wheaton College in
1968, in the midst of that era's student turmoil. Students were
delighted with a man who believed orthodox doctrine and yet

tried to interpret the "worldly" thought and art which surrounded them. Schaeffer then agreed to have his tapes edited into the first few books.

The only books Schaeffer has written intentionally (as opposed to someone adapting his spoken material) are the two connected with his film series, *How Should We Then Live?* and *Whatever Happened to the Human Race? How Should We Then Live?* grew out of a challenge from Billy Zeoli of Gospel Films, who had seen Kenneth Clark's *Civilization* and was convinced an evangelical reply was needed—either from Schaeffer or from Malcolm Muggeridge. *Whatever Happened to the Human Race?* was the brainchild of Franky Schaeffer, not yet thirty, who produced and directed it. It dealt specifically with the three topics of abortion, euthanasia, and infanticide, and featured Schaeffer and Dr. C. Everett Koop of Philadelphia (who eventually became the United States Surgeon General).

How Should We Then Live? set an all-time record in number of bookings for its distributor, Gospel Films, and the $12.95 book coasted atop the religious best-sellers list for months.

Reflecting on his life, Schaeffer seems to take most delight in pointing out the things he pioneered, such as his early fight against racism and his call for Christians to use their wealth compassionately. L'Abri spearheaded a model of community long before radical Christians took up the cause. There was considerable sacrifice involved in the early days of L'Abri: the Schaeffers' open-door policy resulted in ruined wedding presents, cigarette burns in the rug, torn sheets, and vomit stains.

As for his contributions to thought, Schaeffer speaks most proudly of two messages. First, his dual stress of orthodoxy and the need for love and community. He says now he wishes he had stressed specific applications, such as arguments against racism and for distributed wealth. Second, his encouragement of Christians to operate as whole persons within all of culture, giving them a framework for interpreting books, painting, music, and movies.

Schaeffer's system of thought derives from the "antithesis" which he stresses so often: that if a statement is true, the opposite of that statement cannot be true. In personal contacts

Schaeffer attempts to furrow backwards until a person admits what his presuppositions are. He will then develop them logically until the person sees the contradiction in his conclusions. To Schaeffer "no non-Christian can be consistent with the logic of his presuppositions."

In other words, start with a presupposition that the world came about by chance. Schaeffer would prod you, intellectually, to conclude that humans cannot have meaning and that none of our actions make any difference in the world. There is no "outside force" to be accountable to. To Schaeffer, a person who starts with presuppositions that exclude God must become "an atheist in religion, an irrationalist in philosophy, and completely immoral in the wider sense." Schaeffer is at his best in finding contemporary examples of people who admit those presuppositions and conclusions but fail to live consistently with them. For example, Jean-Paul Sartre asserted there is no basis for ethical judgments of right and wrong, yet he broke his own principles by denouncing French treatment of Algeria on moral grounds.

"Pre-evangelism" is the term Schaeffer uses to describe this process of bringing a person to see the logical result of his own presuppositions. Thereafter, Schaeffer presents the Christian alternative, and shows how the Christian conception of a world created by an intelligent designer makes more sense.

A doctoral candidate at Yale, Thomas V. Morris, analyzed the philosophical roots of Schaeffer's thoughts in the book, *Francis Schaeffer's Apologetics: A Critique*, concluding that Schaeffer's approach is really a jazzed-up version of the argument from design. Morris is sympathetic to most of Schaeffer's basic premises, but dislikes his generalizing, sweeping style.

Schaeffer sees a huge rupture in the history of thought cracking open about the time of Hegel, who rejected the antithesis mode of thinking in favor of synthesis. Søren Kierkegaard took Hegel's synthetic approach and applied it to the realm of theology, thus becoming, in Schaeffer's words, "the father of all modern existential thought, both secular and theological." The natural world of the visible and created began to swallow up the unseen world. We can only be sure, say the moderns, of the seen world. The unseen world is not known through reason: it is known through irrational "leaps of faith."

Schaeffer does not like leaps of faith, at least in doctrine. He believes doctrine must derive from a carefully reasoned, step-by-step approach based on the verbal revelation God has given in the Bible. Thus he downplays the nonrational (not irrational) aspects of the gospel. Schaeffer seems to rely on the power of reasoning, as if the only way a person can come to Christ is by arguing himself into the Kingdom, even though many of the gospel's most salient features—unearned grace and unmerited sacrifice, for example—would not be arrived at on the basis of logic from natural revelation.

Where in Schaeffer's system is the *Sehnsucht*, the sense of longing that provided the motif for C. S. Lewis's conversion? One wonders how Schaeffer would respond to a person who came to an emotional (not propositional) awareness of good and evil through reading Tolkien or Tolstoy; would his apprehension of a "first-order, existential" experience be rejected because of its weak epistemology? Or could it too lead him toward Christ? C. S. Lewis, certainly a rational thinker, startled the intellectual world with his premise that the Romantic movement (not Hegel's synthesis or the Renaissance) caused the most profound shift in recent history; yet Schaeffer seems to sidestep that area entirely.

Unlike some apologists, Schaeffer does not restrict his inquiry to the field of knowledge. He is a preacher also, and devotes equal time to the practical application of how the church can and should reveal the holiness and love of God. "I'm sick and tired of dusty apologetics," he says. "To my mind apologetics is not a safe system to live in. Apologetics should lead people to Christ and to a greater comprehension of the Lordship of Christ in the whole spectrum of life."

Schaeffer's main weaknesses result from this dual role he has accepted: that of evangelist and apologist. He believes so sincerely in the force of what he's presenting that, to him, the arguments compel agreement. He uses phrases describing the Christian answer as being a "logically necessary conclusion" rather than a "probable conclusion" or "plausible conclusion." And, searching for illustrations from modern culture to demonstrate his points, he passes over hundreds of examples that wouldn't demonstrate the point. He is a dramatist. He speaks in italics. He makes such statements as, "Picture the line between reason and non-reason as a solid concrete wall with barbed wire in the middle charged with ten thousand volts of electricity. Then you can begin to understand how there can be no interchange between the lower story with reason which leads to despair and the upper story of hope without reason."

Naturally, some Christian philosophers and theologians fidget when they realize Schaeffer has just placed some of their favorite mentors, such as Barth and Kierkegaard, on the wrong side of the concrete wall. As Jack Rogers commented, "Schaeffer lumps Rousseau, Kant, Hegel, and Kierkegaard together. His characterizations of their thought are almost unrecognizable with reference to either their own works or standard textbook treatments of them. . . . One is soon tempted to defend a philosopher simply because he has been unfairly caricatured by Schaeffer, even when one is in reality as critical of him as Schaeffer is—but for quite different reasons."

Schaeffer's confident, panoramic assertions have gained him both notability and notoriety. He has had an incredible impact on young evangelicals who are now likely to confront their teachers with such befuddling questions as: "Let's see, did that composer write before or after the line of despair?"

Sometimes his prophet's mantle causes him to stumble, as in the late sixties when he predicted that the New Left in America would grow "stronger and more violent and more disruptive" and "society itself will move toward chaos."

Yet in many ways Schaeffer has stayed consistent with his presuppositions about what his role should be. Sometimes he delights in calling himself an "old-fashioned evangelist," and one gets the distinct impression that a child who accepts Christ in his little chapel in Switzerland gives him more pleasure than all the brilliant students whose theoretical discussions keep him up so late.

To many sophisticated non-Christians, who are not atheistic existentialists, and who live fulfilled, hopeful lives, oblivious to the line of despair, this strange man with the aura of the Alps about him must appear to be a relic. They go on their way, still benefiting from the moraine of Christian civilization, still reading Dostoyevsky and listening to Mozart masses played by the

Chicago Symphony, still celebrating familial love during holi-days. It is precisely those people who make Francis Schaeffer so intense, so pessimistic, so sober. They are living, he believes, an absolute lie to their presuppositions. They are teetering on the brink of cosmic choices, yet they refuse to face the evidence. He has given his life to try to convince them.

CHAPTER SEVEN

Evangelical Prophet: Francis Schaeffer

Question: Many Christian leaders have tried unsuccessfully to maintain the respect and enthusiasm of young people over a long period of time. But you have succeeded. Why?

Answer: First of all, different people have different qualities and gifts from the Lord. Having said this, I think there are some human elements.

I have dealt with the questions of the developing contemporary scene and haven't gotten stuck back at the point of my own studies when I was a young man, the way some people seem to do. One reason for this is that I was not raised as a Christian and I went through a period when I was agnostic. I became a Christian at eighteen simply through reading my own Bible after reading a lot of philosophy. Therefore I think my own conversion is conducive to thinking in modern terms.

Also, I have had a continuing education, not just from the books that I read but from the many, many people that I talk to. So often Christians don't listen to what the other person says; they just present the Christian position. I've always tried to listen to people who have come from all over the world and from all kinds of disciplines. When young people come to me they find empathy for the simple reason that I don't write off their questions, intellectually or otherwise, and just give them a formula. I really try to deal with the question.

Question: Some of your critics admit that what you've just said is true within the context of L'Abri. When you are with someone in person, you do understand and empathize with their questioning. On the other hand, they say, in your writings—on the cold, dispassionate black and white page—when you deal with people like Karl Barth, for example, that same sort of true listening doesn't occur. There you have a tendency to categorize and typecast people. Do you agree?

Answer: No, I really don't. When you're not writing twenty-six books about Karl Barth, you have to make summaries and, in general, my summaries are correct. Now everybody makes mistakes—I'm sure I've made some—but I would say that I've tried to treat other thinkers compassionately.

In the type of writing I do, I must summarize; I can't possibly deal with all the nuances. So I try to find the central things they've said and the results they've had and present them. I always hold my breath because I know certain nuances would sound different if I were talking for two hours instead of writing on one page.

Question: When *How Should We Then Live?* was breaking sales records, your publisher took out a full-page ad in the *New York Times*, asking, "Why is the secular media ignoring this book?" Does it disappoint you that the secular media has not given coverage to your thought?

Answer: Yes, in a way, because I have tried to write my books to two audiences, the Christians and the non-Christians. The first publisher I offered a book to turned it down because, he said, it seemed directed at both audiences. I was sure books could be written and directed at both audiences, and this has proved to be true. Many non-Christians, whom Christianity wouldn't normally reach, have been touched and even changed.

I'm disappointed about media, because I'd like to see a big impact for the Lord in that world. In order to be accepted in the secular media area, you generally have to be within their framework, and I'm outside of it. But I don't know anyone who has really taken a clear Christian position who has been more widely accepted in the secular area.

Question: In the evangelical world, at least, you have become a media figure with people bidding for your book contracts and audiences of seven thousand packing auditoriums, when you've been accustomed to a room of thirty people discussing issues. Has that been a difficult adjustment for you?

Answer: It hasn't really, because I believe it is just an extension of my previous work. The Lord gave us something that none of us were sure could occur: atmosphere in the midst of those seven thousand which I found just as intimate as speaking to a hundred people in our chapel at L'Abri.

As far as the actual commercial side of it, you have to live in the world you're in. And this is the world we live in, in the same way supermarkets are in our generation. You might wish that the Christian booksellers' business was a different business than it is in our present day. But if you're going to publish books, you have to publish them in a setting that exists and not one that doesn't exist.

Question: Do you think that you have been substantially changed by all that's happened?

Answer: I've thought and prayed about this. I don't see changes. Far more important than my own opinion is that of my friends who would be very honest, and they don't seem to find any change either. Now, who knows? I have to wait to talk to the Lord on Judgment Day to be sure.

Question: Your wife very vividly describes your compassion for people. You care for people, and you listen to them intently. Have you always had this quality?

Answer: I think it is a gift.

Question: Was it present before you were a Christian? Were you drawn toward people?

Answer: I don't think so. Neither was my intellectual interest. I got rotten grades until I became a Christian, and after that I always studied to try to excel. I graduated magna cum laude from Hampden-Sydney College even though in high school I barely made it.

I know I have an analytical mind, and one thing I've learned in a long lifetime is that you don't meet many people who have really analytical minds. This I had before I was a Christian. In fact, I became a Christian after analyzing the liberalism I was hearing preached on one side and the philosophy I was reading on the other.

But I really believe that my ability to sit and talk with one person or seven thousand and answer the questions the way I answer them, covering the intellectual spectrum, is as much a gift of God as anything, and I think the Lord can take it away. As long as that gift is useful in this world, I'm thankful to have it.

Since I've had cancer we've realized more than ever before how God has used our work. Professors in law write, "After all my law studies it was reading your books that made me understand the modern framework of law." Or people in medicine write, "The whole discussion of medical ethics fell into place."

Question: Could you summarize the crucial thinkers who set you going on the way you've ended up, even back in college days?

Answer: Literally hundreds of people have influenced my thought. But certain key people made a real difference in my thinking. It goes all the way back to my junior high school days when I had just one art teacher. I came from a family which was not interested in art at all. She opened the door for me to an interest in art.

Then I had a professor in college, my philosophy professor, who was brilliant. I was his favorite student, because I think I probably was the only student in the class who understood him and stimulated him. He used to invite me down at night to sit around his pot-bellied stove and just discuss. He and I ended up in two very different camps. He became committed to neo-orthodox thinking, but he was very important in my intellectual development.

Question: What historical people?

Answer: I tried to study the whole spectrum of the historic Christian background, specifically out of the Reformation; so I come from a Reformed background by choice. Then I went to Westminster for two years and to Faith Seminary. Cornelius Van Til and Allan MacRae of Biblical Theological Seminary stirred my intellectual thought. Those who are trying to minimize me try to link my thinking only into the Princeton thinking of Hodge and Warfield and so on. A careful reading of my works shows that, although I am very thankful for those men and their day of history, I don't believe they were facing the same problems we are facing in our day. My theological position would be similar to theirs, but our respective presentations are necessarily different.

Question: Because of the breadth of fields that you try to cover, are you mostly limited to secondary sources? There's no way you could encompass music, art, philosophy, literature, science, etc., through primary sources.

Answer: Secondary sources are very important to me, of course. On the other hand, I try to keep up on primary things I think are crucial, so that when I read a secondary source I have a sound basis of judgment.

Also, you must realize that I do not work in isolation. L'Abri is not myself; it is made up of a group of scholars. The outstanding example, I guess, is Hans Rookmaaker, whom I met first when he was still a student. Both he and I say that we have kicked stuff around for so long that in large areas, including art, we would hesitate to say who thought of an idea first. So I haven't worked in isolation. I think anybody who searches for only one or two people to explain my positions and my attitudes is pursuing a hopeless task.

Question: Have any of your major views significantly changed in the last decade—I mean, really abrupt reversals?

Answer: If I thought for a couple of days I might think of something. Not basic ones, I think. I've made tremendous shifts in details. But I think not in major views.

Question: At what point, then, was your basic framework developed?

Answer: Theologically, it was developed all the way back before I went to seminary. When I went to Hampden-Sydney College, the Bible professor, the college president, and the college chaplain were outstanding Christians. But I never would have had the equipment or the content to write the books I've written and deal with the people I deal with across such a wide area if I had remained in the United States. I think going to Europe was providential; it allowed a wider intellectual framework from people coming from all over the world.

People often say, "Why didn't you come and help your own country?" But Edith and I have often said we think we've been greater help to the United States by having gone to Europe.

Question: Do you read in other languages?

Answer: No. And it's been a limitation. My family is all bilingual (French), but I'm not.

Question: As your role has changed over the years, do you think you have been subjected to new, specific temptations?

Answer: Yes, a great danger of spiritual pride has arisen as I deal with large numbers and with so many people reading the books. But then I quickly counteract that by saying I've never seen greater spiritual pride in my life than when somebody was elected president of the Sunday school class with three people in it. Pride is something inside you; mere size doesn't change the danger of it. I believe Satan is playing chess against me and against you and he is clever enough to play it on the existential board we're living on at the moment.

Question: Let's shift to politics. Your writings imply that democracy is the outgrowth of Christian principles of society. Are you committed to democracy as the ideal form of government, or are you just as comfortable in some cultures with very different forms of government?

Answer: When you talk about democracy you have to define it. It doesn't mean you can't have a king. It doesn't have to take the form it takes in the United States. Switzerland doesn't have a strong president: a council of seven rotates, and most Swiss people don't even know who's the current president. So I'm not talking about a specific form of democracy. If you're asking about just the concept of democracy—responsibility being invested in the people, or checks and balances, or *lex rex* rather than *rex lex*—then, yes, I think this is an outgrowth of Christianity.

Question: Some Christians believe models of communism, though not classical Marxism, could be acceptable to Christians and could be adaptable forms of government for other cultures. Do you agree?

Answer: If by communism you mean somewhat more economic control by the state, then, sure, that would be acceptable in certain circumstances. But the word communism has a very strict definition today. The philosophy developed by Marx, Engels, and Lenin brings forth oppression as naturally as the Reformation of Christianity brought forth "law is king." The word communism means that specific materialistic philosophy.

If on the other hand you ask, "Is it necessary to equate democracy with the exact economic situation we have?"—absolutely not. A perfect example is Switzerland. When Switzerland socialized the railroads, did this mean it became a non-capitalistic country? Not at all. It is more capitalistic than the United States. When we socialized the postal system in the United States did this mean that we gave up capitalism or democracy? Absolutely not.

At the moment we are a very different kind of democracy than was visualized by Jefferson. Back then they visualized an elitist group, and our electoral college, for example, endures as a hangover from their ideas. But I believe Christianity leads increasingly away from that to the kind of thing we have now.

Question: Are you a pacifist?

Answer: No, very strenuously no. I hate war with all my heart. But we live in a fallen world, and I think you have to take this into account.

Question: Would you support any revolutionary movements, such as in Africa or in Indochina?

Answer: Oh, sure, I would in certain circumstances. To me, the right of revolution is a part of the democratic process. You must remember I am a radical in this sense. Most people don't realize that.

Question: Would you support armed intervention in a place like Cambodia, or Albania, for the purpose of bringing liberty?

Answer: We live in a very complex world. I'm not hedging. I'm really not. But I discuss this with congressmen and senators, and all kinds of people. And none of this is theoretical.

In this complicated world you have to realize that you can't do everything. But on the other hand, I do believe that at certain points of history it is an exhibition of non-Christian lack of love not to use what is at one's disposal to help other people in their extremities. The monstrous situation in Germany in World War II is an example of a need for outside force.

Question: Are any such monstrous situations facing us now?

Answer: Yes, and I'm worried, because I think the world is going to face the most monstrous situation ever in the role of modern Russian power. It's larger than Hitler's Germany.

I hate all forms of totalitarianism. The political liberals always look at the left with rose-colored glasses in contrast to the right. The biggest example of this tendency is the one that everybody ought to have recognized before Solzhenitsyn came on the scene. The liberals saw the monstrousness of what Hitler was doing almost immediately, but most of these people did not acknowledge what Stalin was doing until *thirty years later*. It's the same with China and Mao. People who are totally neutral have estimated that Mao probably killed more people in taking over power in China than Stalin and Hitler put together.

Now I would just say that in our present circumstances we're facing an obvious confrontation of power. And fortunately, some people are beginning to speak up.

Question: In the film series you draw parallels between our current crisis and the decline of previous civilizations, and you give a lot of warnings about trends in our own civilization. Doesn't the nuclear moat around the United States introduce a brand new element in this decline of civilization? Because, regardless of internal forces, we have the capacity to destroy the rest of the world.

Answer: Yes, we are now living on the possibility of blowing up the whole planet, which makes the whole situation more overwhelming.

Before I continue I must emphasize again that I could never be construed as right wing, so what I'm going to say mustn't be put in that context. I hate the loss of freedom whether it comes from the right or the left.

How Should We Then Live? built up to a climax against authoritarian government itself as such. I hate authoritarian structure in any form—in church, in the state—and I haven't practiced it in my own family with my kids. I believe we are facing a perilous situation today. Churchill was right when he said, after the war, that the only reason the Russian armies were no longer advancing was because America had supremacy with the atom bomb.

Up through the Cuban crisis, the United States had the preponderance of power; so therefore the nuclear situation was a plus for us. At the present time it's a toss-up who has nuclear supremacy. If Russia gains the nuclear supremacy, whether

America will be blasted off the face of earth, I don't know, but certainly in this present alignment China will be.

I could be entirely wrong, but my own conclusion after talking to people in centers of power is that nuclear power now is overestimated. We've reached a stalemate, and I think what will come next will be determined not as much by nuclear weapons as by more conventional methods. I don't think the impetus is an outgrowth of communism as such; it's a blend of Lenin's concept of power and, behind that, "Mother Russia."

Question: It's enlightening to see how Russia capitalizes on that by using Cuba. They could not get away with intervention in Africa by their own soldiers. So they hire mercenaries, like their own French Foreign Legion.

Answer: Exactly right. I doubt they plan to invade Europe. I think they intend to use their military might as a political weapon to achieve their purpose without the necessity of armed intervention.

Question: You mean Western European countries will become communist through political means?

Answer: No, we'll come to a showdown and the result will be the reverse of the Cuban missile situation. The enormity of what would be involved for poor Europe will cause them to take a lesser stand politically. Then will come another political stand. . . .

Question: In the same way the Arabs changed Europe's foreign policy toward Israel with the threat of an oil embargo?

Answer: Yes! Overnight. To pursue this, I think Russia has a several-pronged program which shows great brilliance and is consistent with Lenin. The first prong is their armies; they've stalemated us with nuclear power. Then they have the hardcore of the political parties in western Europe. And then they have the extension of military power with the Cuban and Vietnamese forces. And also, I am convinced that they support the terrorists in the West, even though the terrorists may be against the communistic parties. I think Russia supports anything that causes upheaval and chaos and breakdown in the West. So they have a many-pronged, yet united, program.

You asked originally if I saw any monstrous situation in the world today. Boy, oh, boy, do I. My brothers in Christ, whom I love very much, who are pacifists—I just think they're mistaken.

Question: Have you worked out theories about how the trends of civilization which you trace in your books and your own view of prophecy come together?

Answer: No. I take eschatology seriously, of course. But I think the Bible warns us that we can't be absolutely sure by any means that we live in any specific portion of that eschatological program. Let me state it another way. I believe I should live every day of my life as though Christ may come back before I die. But at the same time I don't believe I can ever say I know that I am watching the fulfillment of the eschatological situation. I'm curious, and holding the very strong views I do on eschatology, naturally I'm intrigued. But I don't allow it to shape my practical and political feelings.

Question: I get the impression that a lot of Christians would vote for the Antichrist if they knew who he was, just to hasten Christ's return. But in the Arab situation, the fact that Israel may in fact be God's chosen people and may eventually fit into some theories of eschatology really should have no bearing on the morality of how you treat the Arabs or Palestinians.

Answer: I quite agree. If I were President of the United States, I must say, I wouldn't make my decisions here in a certain historical situation on the basis that scriptural prophecy would make certain decisions mandatory.

Question: One of your more recent emphases is the disparity of wealth and a Christian's responsibility in an affluent society. The theory and scriptural basis are fairly common in the Christian world today. But the practicality—how this affects me in my decision on what car to buy, what house to buy, how many pairs of pants to own, whether to have investments—is very complex. Do you have any practical advice?

Answer: When I was a pastor in western Pennsylvania one of the big discussions was whether you could be spiritual and have life insurance. I emphasized then that the church cannot legislate you. The Bible doesn't and therefore we cannot give absolutes. All we can do is produce principles, and then the individual must decide under the leadership of the Holy Spirit how to apply those principles to the situation. Conceivably the Holy

Spirit could lead one person to apply them one way, and another person to apply them slightly differently and they would be equally right.

I've stood for a compassionate use of accumulated wealth, and I get shot at by both sides. The people who want to have all the affluence and never think of compassion don't like my emphasis, but I also get shot at for using the term accumulated wealth, because radical Christians are drifting toward the position that any accumulation of wealth is wrong.

I believe the Bible teaches a right of private property. There are cautions: first, how we get it; second, how we use it. In the New Testament, it is quite clear that Christians had personal property, or they wouldn't have had anything to give when Paul appealed for funds.

I've stressed repeatedly that the church should have two orthodoxies—the orthodoxy of doctrine and the orthodoxy of community. L'Abri was an icebreaker among evangelicals in many senses, including a whole new emphasis on community. But we have made a very strenuous distinction between a commune and community. The commune has more or less taken on the connotation of sharing all goods. L'Abri is not a commune, but a community of families living together in their own homes with their own personalities, their own property, their own direction of their children.

I cannot remember anybody preaching about community when I was younger. And I can't remember anything that would approximate what I would emphasize and what L'Abri would emphasize on the compassionate use of accumulated wealth.

Question: Do you give away a lot of your income?

Answer: Well, first of all, understand that Edith and I have turned all our earnings over to L'Abri. They control our royalties.

Question: Do they contribute heavily to underdeveloped countries?

Answer: Individuals do. But L'Abri is a very costly program because we take people in and charge them very little.

Question: Your book, *The New Super-Spirituality*, referred to Christian competitiveness. Isn't there a new danger among certain groups to build competitive pride about how poorly they live and how much they give away? That's exactly what caused the downfall of Ananias and Sapphira: they were trying to be super-spiritual.

Answer: I think we have to consciously live within two Christian realities: the fallen world and our finiteness. Nobody can give away everything. It's always proportionate. Now I would say the proportion must be left up to the Holy Spirit to lead.

We have no right to set absolutes unless they can be shown directly from Scripture. Nobody has a right to tell me that spirituality means that I should get four thousand dollars a year instead of five, or whether I should buy my children a bicycle. That's my business before the Lord.

Question: Looking back over all the things that you have done, which do you feel best about?

Answer: The first would be speaking historic Christianity in a way that can be understood by contemporary people and can be shown to be relevant to them, so that many of them become Christians.

The other thing would be the emphasis that being a Christian is not some obscure thing in the upper levels of spirituality, but encompasses the whole of life. Christians have begun to realize that Christianity meant something in the arts and culture and law in a way that a lot of them had never thought of before.

I stand theologically in the stream of historic Christianity—the early church and the Reformation—so I haven't said anything new. But I seem, by the grace of God, to have been able to say these things to contemporary people in a way they have comprehended.

Question: Some Christians have come away from you confused about how they should relate to the arts. You refer to a "line of despair" which implies that the *forms* used by modern artists and musicians and writers are somehow tainted or immoral. The only way I can function as a Christian artist, people have said to me, is to leapfrog back a century and pick up old forms.

Answer: Oh, no. Maybe I didn't protect myself sufficiently. The people who have been with me in L'Abri don't think this way—but I can see how the people who just come in contact with the books could think that.

Technique is neutral, and you can't say that a certain technique is godly or ungodly. But there is a form of the world's spirit for every generation, and this infiltrates all kinds of things, including Christian thinking, unless we consciously reject it.

In art, techniques have been born of the really brilliant people in those fields trying to find a vehicle to express their world view. I don't believe that these people necessarily sit down in the Cafe Voltaire in Zurich, where dadaism was born, for example, and construct these things. I would just say that a person's world view, consciously or unconsciously, naturally shows itself with some consistency in the totality of life. Be careful here, because they're still made in the image of God, whether they know it or not; so there are brakes. But in general what I've said is true.

Because modern forms of art were brought forth in order to express a certain world view, it therefore becomes very tricky for the young Christian artist or writer. The techniques are neutral, not godly or ungodly. But it's easier to produce a world view through the vehicle conceived to express it than it is to convey another world view. Therefore I am not opposed to modern forms of art, but I think you do have to keep in mind why the form was produced.

T. S. Eliot is a perfect example. He didn't write old-fashioned poetry after he became a Christian, but his poetry was different. The form of *The Wasteland* wouldn't fit his later poems, though it fitted his world view magnificently when he wrote *The Wasteland*.

Question: Can you think of any examples like that in music?

Answer: Music is the hardest of all to discuss, and it's the one which I always approach with the greatest hesitancy. You can't visualize music or examine it in the same way in which you can examine something on the printed page, or on a canvas. Yet nevertheless we see the same general things in music that are more easily pointed out in writing or poetry or painting.

Question: Of the various disciplines, I think the popular culture has been most resistant to new classical forms of music. When the Chicago Symphony plays John Cage the people boo. I don't know if they can ever get over that.

Answer: I don't think they should get over it. By the time you get to John Cage, in contrast to somebody like Stravinsky, he is

126 / Open Windows

writing a philosophic statement. One of my quarrels with modern art is that it's too philosophical. I have the same quarrel with it that I have with much evangelical art. It isn't art; it's a tract. Propaganda. People like Marcel du Champs and John Cage didn't set out to make works of art, they set out to make philosophic statements.

Question: You make specific interpretations of artists. For instance, when you criticize the Salvador Dali crucifixion painting as implying a lack of reality, have you researched that? Have you found a statement by Salvador Dali that says his technique was intended to imply historical questions about Jesus or are you just inferring that?

Answer: Curiously enough, in a *Playboy* interview, Salvador Dali said that he now was reading the modern scientists and coming to realize that the earth was made up not basically of mass, but of energy. Then he leaped into the fact that we should have a spiritual representation in our art. So *Playboy*, of all things, has been very helpful with Salvador Dali.

Question: That introduces an interesting subject: the philosophic movement within science for a view of the universe at its core being irrational rather than rational. You don't seem comfortable with these new findings, such as the Heisenberg Indeterminacy Principle.

Answer: Certainly I realize the older Newtonian concepts have to be modified. But even when we're dealing with the very small, say in a cyclotron, we are still dealing on the basis of cause and effect in the larger area, regardless of what's happening in the smaller area. If we didn't deal on the basis of cause and effect, nobody could build the cyclotron.

There is a difference between not accepting the Cartesian concept that in our human finiteness we can plot every graph mathematically, and jumping into the area of irrationality. The building of the cyclotron is an absolute proof that the very men who are producing it are denying irrationality by their own actions.

Question: What do they say to that when you confront them?

Answer: Nobody's ever answered me. There's sudden silence.

Question: You mean you have sat, one to one like this, with physicists and asked this question?

Answer: Yes, sure. Amazingly, a great number of them have never thought it through, perhaps because people are playing many, many games instead of thinking the big questions. Their game can be knocking one tenth of one second off a downhill run in the Swiss Alps. It also can show up in a highly disciplined science where one focuses on a very small area of reality and then never thinks of the big question.

Question: I assume you're familiar with Niebuhr's principles of Christ and culture. How good is it for us to redeem culture? In some ways is it not better for Christians to be a minority, a counterculture?

Answer: The ideal would be if I could wave a wand and have a Christian consensus where you wouldn't have a confusion of church and state. I believe that's what the founders of America hoped for. You wouldn't have a state church but you would have a Christian consensus. Therefore you really would be influencing the culture overwhelmingly.

Question: When in history has that occurred?

Answer: Never. There's no golden age. I'm tired of people who would try to make me say the Reformation was a golden age. It was anything but a golden age.

But the United States when I was young through the Twenties and Thirties showed basically a Christian consensus. It was, of course, poorly applied in certain areas, such as race or compassionate use of accumulated wealth.

Question: What has happened since that time? Has the Christian consensus shrunk in percentage? Has it grown less vocal? Or would you say the worldly philosophies have taken sway and leveled its impact?

Answer: All of those factors. Humanism has come to its natural conclusion and we now live in a secularized society. You can teach atheism in our schools but you can't sing Christmas carols. And secular presuppositions now control law, education, all these things.

The church follows the same curve slightly later. Most of our large denominations allow liberal theology to dominate the seminaries and the bureaucracies. They take on exactly the same thought forms as the secular world, because to my mind liberal theology is only humanism in Christian terminology.

So those two trends have come together: secularism and a church dominated by the same basic philosophy.

Question: You are now introduced on stage as an intellectual muscle man and people come knowing that, ready to attack you. Your book jacket blurbs call you "the missionary to the intellectual" and other labels that probably embarrass you. How do these things affect your self-concept? Do you get nostalgic for those old, first days in Europe, thirty years ago?

Answer: It all seems very unreal to me, which I think is a protection that the Lord has given.

Question: I've heard people snipe at you by saying you feed the image of the wise man on the mountain—for example, by wearing knickers to go along with the role.

Answer: The reason I wear knickers is just because I have found them comfortable. I used them first for climbing and cross-country skiing and so I gradually got into the habit of wearing them.

Question: But when you go to a U.S. ministers' conference—it becomes a statement. Why are you standing apart from the norm?

Answer: I suppose I found it helpful the first times I came over in the sixties. I've never thought of it before until you just asked me. When I went to a place like Wheaton, it gave me an edge by setting me off from the stereotype. So in a way I wasn't what they were used to, and of course in my thinking I wasn't.

Question: If I had asked you fifteen years ago, "Are you ever going to write a book?" what would you have said?

Answer: No. I'm interested in *talking* to people. But after lecturing, for example, at Harvard, suddenly these Harvard students, almost none of whom were Christians, gave me a standing ovation. One of the professor's wives turned to Edith and said, "I've been at Harvard for thirty years and have never seen a standing ovation." It was true at M.I.T., and other places. But I still wouldn't have thought of going beyond the individual conversation, the lectures with give-and-take afterwards. In those days I had more energy, so I'd stay up till 2 or 3 o'clock in the morning.

Question: One critic who observed you in Los Angeles said that probably most of the people in the auditorium did not understand what you were saying in the films or in person. The audience applauded your seeming expertise, but this critic really doubted that they went out with changed perceptions.

Answer: I would just say that he ought to read the letters that have come. If you preach a straight gospel sermon, part of the people aren't going to understand that. A remarkable number of people have understood remarkably much, to such an extent that it has changed their lives. I think the critic is mistaken.

Question: In the film series, at what point were you trying to do a respectable scholarly analysis of history and culture, couched in terms of objectivity, and at what point did you have the motivation of evangelism? Aren't those two motives dichotomous?

Answer: I believe that Christianity is true. And it's true in the totality of truth. Now it doesn't give you the answer to quantum physics. But I believe that the closer you can come to truth, objective truth, the more Christianity will be substantiated. I don't see any dichotomy.

In the beginning of the book *How Should We Then Live?* I say this is not an exhaustive study of Western history and culture. Nobody could write a book like that. It is selective, but every history book is selective. I am so convinced of the truth of Christianity that I see no inherent tension between objectivity and what I think is the purpose of apologetics (that is, getting people to become Christian and Christians to become more deeply endowed with the concept of the Lordship of Christ in our culture and in the whole spectrum of life).

Question: Why do you downplay many of the gross Christian errors throughout history? You do mention some of them, of course, but it surely seems the Thirty Years' War, the Crusades, the Inquisitions, the squelching of science, and events like these had a comparatively lesser part in your film series than they had in history. Did you do that purposely?

Answer: Yes. In the first place there is the space limitation. Second, there are some things to which you must devote a huge number of pages or frames of a film, or you'd better not touch them. The Crusades are a perfect example. I think they were destructive. I don't think they had any place in a real Christian framework. But what are you going to do with them in a book or a film like this? If you ask me to discuss them, I'll spend half an hour talking to you about the Crusades.

Question: Your methodology, not in person, but in writing, can appear to be rationalistic. And yet, your concept of the Fall must include the fact that human reason also is fallen. How can you build on such a rationalistic base?

Answer: I'm convinced that the Bible teaches something between a natural theologian such as Aquinas and a materialist who cannot count on human reason. We are fallen, and there's no way to start from the finite and move to the infinite—we'll draw the wrong conclusions. But human reason still functions and, as Paul argues in Romans 1, the evidence is adequate. So adequate that we can be called disobedient if we don't bow to it.

Every so often a writer comes along who simply creates a new creative category. In my opinion, Annie Dillard did just that with Pilgrim at Tinker Creek, *for which she was awarded the Pulitzer Prize.*

If you ask what the book is about, a loyal Dillard fan will stare at you vacantly. About? Well, a woman takes walks in the woods and sees tadpoles and water striders and things, and relates unusual facts about trees and creeks. Not much of a plot, really. Yet behind her observations lies a natural theology that has not been attempted with such ambition since perhaps Joseph Butler.

Annie Dillard is a Christian who lives in a post-Voltaire, post-Darwin age of naturalistic skepticism and yet somehow avoids the blinders of that age. She knows that nature contains, in Rudolf Otto's phrase, Mysterium tremendum. *Even in a broken and twisted world she sees enough to leave her breathless.*

When I read Pilgrim *and later* Holy the Firm, *I knew I had to meet Annie Dillard. Before long I was sitting in her office on Puget Sound conducting the interview which follows. For those unacquainted with Annie Dillard, I have interspersed appropriate selections from her work.*

CHAPTER EIGHT

A Face Aflame: Annie Dillard

Question: Annie, when I mention you to my friends, I get one of two reactions: either a sigh of appreciation from a fervent admirer or a puzzled "Who?" It seems most evangelicals are in the second category.

Answer: Well, I admit I am consciously addressing the unbeliever in my books, though I have great empathy for evangelicals. I was raised Presbyterian, in Pittsburgh, and during my development I had only one short fling of rebellion against God.

For four consecutive summers I had gone to a fundamentalist church camp in the country. We sang Baptist songs and had a great time—it gave me a taste for abstract thought. But I grew sick of people going to church just to show off their clothes, so I quit the church. Instead of quietly dropping away, I wanted to make a big statement; so I marched into the assistant minister's office. I gave him my spiel about how much hypocrisy there was in the church. This kind man replied, "You're right, honey, there is."

Before leaving, I said, "By the way, I have to write a senior paper for the school—do you have any C. S. Lewis books?" He gave me an armful and I started a long paper on C. S. Lewis. By the time I finished I was right back in the arms of Christianity. My rebellion lasted a month.

Question: You have gained stature in the publishing world so quickly. It's amusing to be with publishers who think they have the whole literary scene predicted and portrayed on graphs and charts. Then out of nowhere comes a young woman with her first book, which gets the Pulitzer Prize. Were you shocked?

Answer: Sure, but what excited me more was the acceptance of the first chapter from *Pilgrim* for *Harper's* magazine. That day I was happy. I was out playing softball when the phone call came. I ran in, ate an apple very quickly, and called everyone I knew. Twenty-four hours later I got happy all over again. The Pulitzer came much later—over a year later.

Question: You did, however, become a public person suddenly. How did that affect you?

Answer: It was confusing at first. Offers came in from everywhere: offers to write texts for photography books, to write for Hollywood, write ballets and words for songs. And I received hundreds of invitations to speak and teach.

That whole business is a dreadful temptation for an artist. I thought about it, and finally made my choice by turning down an appearance on the *Today* show. Now I give only one reading a year, and virtually no other public appearances. I have chosen to be a writer—and I must stick to that; the craft demands my full energy.

Question: Did you get many personal letters from readers of *Pilgrim?*

Answer: Yes. One man, a professor of theology at a Catholic university, wrote that he resigned his job immediately after reading it. Another woman, a devout Catholic, was a book editor for *The National Observer*. She wrote a very sympathetic, intelligent review for her paper, discussing the religious angle thoroughly. On the same page with the review, the paper ran her obituary; she had died shortly after finishing the review.

Many people who responded with the most warmth were struggling with cancer or some similar burden.

Question: You seem easily moved by people. And yet, you write about them only rarely; you prefer objects and nature. Why? Don't people fascinate you in the same way?

Answer: Oh yes—they do. I just don't think I'm good enough to write about people yet. I'd love to try some day.

There is one church here, so I go to it. On Sunday mornings I quit the house and wander down the hill to the white frame church in the firs. On a big Sunday there might be twenty of us there; often I am the only person under sixty, and feel as though I'm on an archaeological tour of Soviet Russia. The members are of mixed denominations; the minister is a Congregationalist, and wears a white shirt. The man knows God. Once in the middle of the long pastoral prayer of intercession for the whole world—for the gift of wisdom to its leaders, for hope and mercy to the grieving and pained, succor to the oppressed, and God's grace to all—in the middle of this he stopped, and burst out, 'Lord, we bring you these same petitions every week.' After a shocked pause, he continued reading the prayer. Because of this, I like him very much. 'Good morning!' he says after the first hymn and invocation, startling me witless every time, and we all shout back, 'Good Morning!' (Holy the Firm, pp. 57-58).

Question: I have heard that you have come in contact with rigid fundamentalists. How do they affect you?

Answer: I have great respect for them. When I lived in Virginia, I did readings for the blind at a nearby Bible college. Fundamentalists have intense faith. Many educated people think them naive. But fundamentalists know they have chosen the narrow way; they know the social scorn they face.

You must remember, however, my prime audience is the skeptic, the agnostic, not the Christian. Just getting the agnostic to acknowledge the supernatural is a major task.

Question: Your latest book, *Holy the Firm*, differs greatly in structure from *Pilgrim at Tinker Creek*. It's a fraction of the length, more narrative in style, more abstract, more directly theological. Many people consider it less penetrable. What did you hope to accomplish?

Answer: I chose an artistic structure. I decided to write about whatever happened in the next three days. The literary possibilities of that structure intrigued me. On the second day an airplane crashed nearby, and I was back where I had been in *Pilgrim*—grappling with the problem of pain and dying. I had no intention of dealing with that issue at first, but it became unavoidable.

I kept getting stuck. Those forty-three manuscript pages took me fifteen months to write. In *Pilgrim* I would get stuck for three days at a time and I would just plow through. But in *Holy the Firm* the problems were enormous. The question I constantly faced was, "Can it be done?" After the second day's plane crash . . . how could I resolve anything on the third day?

I would have to crank myself up to approach the stack of manuscript pages. Then I'd read what I had written on the last pages and even I couldn't understand it. I don't live on that kind of level.

Question: People who know you through your writings probably assume you do live on that level, don't they?

Answer: Yes, that's an unfortunate error. As a writer, I am less a creator than an audience to the artistic vision. In *Holy the Firm* I even inserted a disclaimer. I said, "No one has ever lived well." I do not live well. I merely point to the vision.

People, holy people, ask me to speak at their monasteries and I write back and say no, keep your vision. In *The Wizard of Oz* there's a giant machine that announces "Dorothy!"; behind the curtain a little man is cranking it and pushing buttons. When the dog pulls back the curtain to expose the little man, the machine says, "Pay no attention to that man behind the curtain! Look at the light show."

So I ask the monks to keep their vision of power, holiness, and purity. We all have glimpses of the vision, but the truth is that no man has ever lived the vision.

Question: How does your own vision penetrate your life? You don't write much about ethics.

Answer: No, I don't write at all about ethics. I try to do right and rarely do. The kind of art I write is shockingly uncommitted—appallingly isolated from political, social, and economic affairs.

There are lots of us here. Everybody writes about politics and social concerns; I don't. I'm not doing any harm.

About five years ago I saw a mockingbird make a straight vertical descent from the roof gutter of a four-story building. It was an act as careless and spontaneous as the curl of a stem or the kindling of a star.

The mockingbird took a single step into the air and dropped. His wings were still folded against his sides as though he were singing from a limb and not falling, accelerating thirty-two feet per second per second through empty air. Just a breath before he would have been dashed to the ground, he unfurled his wings with exact, deliberate care, revealing the broad bars of white, spread his elegant, white-banded tail, and so floated onto the grass. I had just rounded a corner when his insouciant step caught my eye; there was no one else in sight. The fact of this free fall was like the old philosophical conundrum about the tree that falls in the forest. The answer must be, I think, that beauty and grace are performed whether or not we will or sense them. The least we can do is try to be there (Pilgrim at Tinker Creek, pp. 7-8).

Question: You write as an observer, perched on the edge, but also immersed in the world. You ask us to see it with new, enlightened eyes. But how are your powers of observation affected by what has happened to you in the last few years? Can you maintain an innocent gaze when you know you could make a pile of money on your walk through the woods or on your trip to the Galapagos Islands, or even on your visit to the hospital to visit the plane crash victims?

Answer: That's not been a problem. I'd certainly not walk in the woods thinking I'd write a book about it. That would drive me nuts in no time.

Question: In *Holy the Firm*, you lived those three days knowing you'd write a book about them.

Answer: True. I started it as a poem. I merely waited to see what was going to happen and I wasn't looking at my reactions. I simply needed a certain amount of events—whatever might happen—to make a minor point: that days are lived in the mind *and* in the spirit.

Question: In other words, what we perceive happening in a day is really just the surface layer; something much greater and more profound is occurring behind the curtain.

Answer: Yes. How does the world look from within? And that brought in the concept of *Holy the Firm*.

Every day has its own particular brand of holiness for us to discover and worship appropriately. The only way to deal with that was to discover the relationship between time and eternity. That single question interests me artistically more than any other.

If you examine each day, with the events and objects it contains, as a god, you instantly have to conclude there are pagan gods. And if you believe in a holy God—how does he relate to these pagan gods that fill the world? That is exactly the same question as the relationship between time and eternity. Does the holy God bring forth these pagan gods out of his love?

Here I depart from the British rationalists like C. S. Lewis, G. K. Chesterton, and George MacDonald. I am grounded strongly in art and weakly in theology. There is a profound difference between the two fields. If I wanted to make a theological statement I would have hired a skywriter. Instead, I knock myself out trying to do art, and it's not so airtight. It isn't reducible to a sealed system. It doesn't translate so well.

Question: Then that's why in your books you give us both hope and despair, anger and love.

Answer: I guess. I must stay faithful to art. I get in my little canoe and paddle out to the edge of mystery. It is unfortunately true that words fail, reason fails; and all I can do is to create a world which by its internal coherence makes a degree of sense. I can either do that or hush. And then I learn to make statements about that world, to furrow deeper into the mystery.

Every single thing I follow takes me there, to the edge of a cliff. As soon as I start writing, I'm hanging over the cliff again. You can make a perfectly coherent world at the snap of a finger—but only if you don't bother being honest about it.

Question: You seem driven to that mystery. You describe the beauty of nature with such eloquence in *Pilgrim at Tinker Creek*—but just as I'm exulting, you strike me with its terror and injustice.

Answer: As I wrote *Pilgrim*, I kept before me the image of people who are suffering. They were right there in the room as I wrote the book. I could not write a cheerful nature book or a new version of the argument from design—not with a leukemia patient next to me. I had to write for people who are dying or grieving—and that's everybody. I can't write just from my safe position.

When I worked on *Holy the Firm* and the plane went down, I thought, *Oh no, God is making me write about this damn problem of pain again.* I felt I was too young, I didn't know the answer and didn't want to—but again, I had to.

In the Koran, Allah asks, 'The heaven and the earth and all in between, thinkest thou I made them in jest?' It's a good question. What do we think of the created universe, spanning an unthinkable void with an unthinkable profusion of forms? Or what do we think of nothingness, those sickening reaches of time in either direction? If the giant water bug was not made in jest, was it then made in earnest? Pascal uses a nice term to describe the notion of the creator's, once having called forth the universe, turning his back to it: Deus Absconditus. Is this what we think happened? Was the sense of it there, and God absconded with it, ate it, like a wolf who disappears round the edge of the house with the Thanksgiving turkey? 'God is subtle,' Einstein said, 'but not malicious.' Again, Einstein said that 'nature conceals her mystery by means of her essential grandeur, not by her cunning.' It could be that God has not absconded but spread, as our vision and understanding of the universe have spread, to a fabric of spirit and sense so grand and subtle, so powerful in a new way, that we can only feel blindly of its hem. In making the thick darkness, a swaddling band for the sea, God 'set bars and doors' and said, 'Hitherto shalt thou come, but no further.' But have we come even that far? Have we rowed out to the thick darkness, or are we all playing pinochle in the bottom of the boat? (Pilgrim, p. 7).

Question: C. S. Lewis said something like this about nature: you don't go to her to derive your theology. You go to her with your theology and let her fill those words (glory, redemption, love) with meaning.

Answer: I like that.

Question: Yet I get the idea, in *Pilgrim* especially, that you did go to nature to derive your theology.

Answer: In a way, that's true. I approached the whole chaos of nature as if it were God's book. From it I derived symbols and themes that gave me some structures for truth.

Question: But only God can tell you about God. Nature merely tells you about nature. What if something you learned from nature contradicted other revelation?

Answer: If I thought I had to make the choice between God and nature, I would choose God. But I don't think I have to make that choice.

Question: When you studied nature, you came away with a simultaneous sense of awe and horror?

Answer: It can't be reduced to those terms. In *Pilgrim* I wrote about the *via positiva* and the *via negativa*. The rich, full expression of God's love bursts out in all the particulars of nature. Everything burgeons and blossoms—and then comes a devastating flood. There is spring, but also winter. There is intricacy in detail, but also oppressive fecundity as nature runs wild. It all starts collapsing; I see sacrifice and then prayer and everything empties and empties until I'm at the shores of the unknown where I started—except much more informed now.

Question: Chesterton said about nature that it's wrong to refer to her as mother nature. She's really sister nature, a separate, parallel creation to man with all his flaws and inconsistencies. She's half good and half bad.

Answer: Well, I sure as heck deal with that. I don't have a summary sentence for my view. It's all in the books somewhere.

That something is everywhere and always amiss is part of the very stuff of creation. It is as though each clay form had baked into it, fired into it, a blue streak of nonbeing, a shaded emptiness like a bubble that not only shapes its very structure but that also causes it to list and ultimately explode. We could have planned things more mercifully, perhaps, but our plan would never get off the drawing board until we agree to the very compromising terms that are the only ones that being offers.

The world has signed a pact with the devil; it had to. It is a covenant to which every thing, even every hydrogen atom, is bound. The terms are clear; if you want to live, you have to die; you cannot have mountains and creeks without space, and space is a beauty married to a blind man. The blind man is Freedom, or Time, and he does not go anywhere without his great dog Death. The world came into being with the signing of the contract. A scientist calls it the Second Law of Thermodynamics. A poet says, 'The force that through the green fuse drives the flower/Drives my green age.' This is what we know. The rest is gravy (Pilgrim, *pp. 180-181*).

Question: The group you referred to as the British rationalists, notably Lewis, would explain this planet as the condemned planet, an outpost of the universe where evil runs rampant. Perhaps that's why he makes the statement that you can't get your theology from nature. You are on the carbuncle planet and you may come up with a carbuncle theology. Do you view the universe as filled with God's love and the earth as a marred exception?

Answer: That's nuts. We live in the age when we have the photographs of earth from space. Here is one absolutely beautiful sphere floating among the others. There's more beauty in the variety and richness of life here than on the other planets. As an artist, that picture from space has to affect my view.

Question: I'm sure their reference is to worlds in other dimensions, that the holy world is more real than this world.

Answer: Perhaps. But this world merited the Incarnation. If everything is a symbol of spiritual reality, then earth's beauty means something. The classical orthodox definition of beauty is that beauty is the splendor of truth. Beauty and goodness and truth are a triad.

The beauty of this world can't be brushed away. It is true there is sin and pain and suffering, but to call the earth a blot in the universe is evasive. If you carry that through to its conclusion, then God should never have created the world; it was all some horrible mistake.

Question: Lewis uses the analogy of Christ's incarnation as a diver plunging into the depths to rescue a pearl without a glimmer of light and pulling it back into the light.

Answer: Yes—I love that image of God emptying himself.

Question: So we're really back to your own key question of time and eternity. Just how involved is God in this world?

Answer: I believe, often, that nature participates in the essence of God himself and if he removed his loving attention from it for a fraction of a second life would cease.

Question: You referred in *Pilgrim at Tinker Creek* to Heisenberg's Indeterminacy Principle in physics. If randomness is the rule, what part does God play? Isn't it true that this principle strengthens the concept of God the sustainer? If he weren't here, it could literally fall apart at any moment. There must be wisdom behind it.

Answer: And yet you have to be very careful how you state that, because it borders on superstition. I believe that ultimately the people praying in the monasteries are keeping the whole thing going—metaphorically, at least—but there's a huge danger within any religion that it will lapse into superstition.

Question: Do you believe in miracles of the supernatural, nature-interrupting sense?

Answer: Of course. I have no problem with them at all. I'm a long way from agnosticism. I can't imagine now how I could have had a problem with them at one time.

To me the real question is, How in the world can we *remember* God? I like that part of the Bible that ticks off kings as good and bad. Suddenly there comes this one, King Josiah, who orders the temple to be cleaned up and inadvertently discovers the law.

This happens after generations of rulers and following God through the Exodus. Somehow they had forgotten the whole thing, every piece of it. Recognizing that, the king tears his clothes and cries.

A whole nation simply forgot God. We think, how can we forget—we who have seen God? Is it right of God to insist that we wear strings around our fingers to remember him?

This notion of recollection is a pressing spiritual problem—not only how can we remember God, but why does he let us forget? I'm always forgetting God—always, always. That famous prayer, "I will in the course of this day forget thee; forget thou not me" is sometimes thought of as a warm Christian joke. I don't think it is so funny. I think it's exactly what we should be asking.

The secret of seeing is, then, the pearl of great price. If I thought he could teach me to find it and keep it forever I would stagger barefoot across a hundred deserts after any lunatic at all. But although the pearl may be found, it may not be sought. The literature of illumination reveals this above all: although it comes to those who wait for it, it is always, even to the most practiced and adept, a gift and a total surprise. I return from one walk knowing where the killdeer nests in the field by the creek and the hour the laurel blooms. I return from the same walk a day later scarcely knowing my own name. Litanies hum in my ears; my tongue flaps in my mouth Ailinon, alleluia! I cannot cause light; the most I can do is try to put myself in the path of its beam. It is possible, in deep space, to sail on solar wind. Light, be it particle or wave, has force: you rig a giant sail and go. The secret of seeing is to sail on solar wind. Hone and spread your spirit till you yourself are a sail, whetted, translucent, broadside to the merest puff (Pilgrim, *p. 33*).

Question: There is another side of God. One of the scenes in Scripture is Jesus weeping over unreceptive Jerusalem. "Oh that I could gather you under my wings," he says. A very strange statement for an omnipotent God. He has limited his actions on earth, he refuses to coerce.

Answer: I often wonder why God didn't make things clearer, why he spoke in a still, small voice. And I get angry at God when I see so many good people who appear to lack an organ by which they can perceive God. I blame God for that; but that's just the way he chooses to go about things. I often think of God as a fireball—friendly—who just rolls by. If you're lucky you get a slight glimpse of him.

Question: But if you actively look for the fireball he can be found. Nature can be one vehicle, as *Pilgrim* shows.

Answer: The sixteenth-century British mystic named Juliana of Norwich wrote *Revelations of Divine Love,* which I've only had the courage to read once. Its main idea, God's love, is the most threatening of all, because it demands such faith.

Question: You have described yourself as hanging onto the edge of a cliff, grappling. Yet I read a review of *Holy the Firm* that paints you as the predetermined Christian with pat answers. To the reviewer, you were not hanging on the cliff: you were still very much on solid ground and he was over the cliff, unbelieving.

Answer: That's the trouble. Agnostics don't know what in the world is going on. They think religion is safety when in fact *they* have the safety. To an agnostic you have to say over and over again that the fear of death doesn't lead you to love of God. Love of God leads you to fear of death.

Agnostics often think that people run to God because they are afraid of dying. On the contrary, the biblical religion is not a safe thing. People in the Bible understood the transitory nature—the risk—of life better than most people. They weren't using religion as an escape hatch. Faith forces you to a constant awareness of final things. Agnostics don't remember all the time that they're going to die. But Christians do remember. All our actions in this life must be affected by God's point of view.

What can any artist set on fire but his world? What can any people bring to the altar but all it has ever owned in the thin towns or over the desolate plains? What can an artist use but materials, such as they are? What can he light but the short string of his gut, and when that's burnt out, any muck ready to hand?

His face is flame like a seraph's, lighting the kingdom of God for the people to see; his life goes up in the works; his feet are waxen and salt. He is holy and he is firm, spanning all the long gap with the length of his love, in flawed imitation of Christ on the cross stretched both ways unbroken and thorned. So must the work be also, in touch with, in touch with, in touch with; spanning the gap, from here to eternity, home (Holy the Firm, p. 72).

PART THREE

The Language of Faith

When asked what specifically brought them to a relationship with God, many Christians will cite a moving sermon, a praying family, an evangelistic meeting or an acquaintance with the Bible. I would have to answer that nature and classical music were decisive factors in awakening my spiritual life. I grew up in an environment clotted with key phrases, memorized Bible verses, and prescribed spiritual activities. Before long, I could no longer distinguish a true prayer from a performance prayer or an authentic act from a hypocritical one.

In a sense, I had been vaccinated against spiritual truth; I had heard it all before, and learned to reject it. About that time, something began to stir in me: an appreciation for beauty. I would take long walks in the Carolina pine forests, follow butterflies across fields, stare at the Milky Way creasing the heavens. And late at night I would slip into the college chapel and play Chopin, Schubert, and Beethoven on the concert grand.

It is a terrible thing to be grateful and have no one to thank, to be awed and have no one to worship. Gradually, very gradually, I came back to the castoff faith of my childhood. Rather, I was drawn back by the Sehnsucht, or sense of longing for, in C. S. Lewis' words, "a scent of a flower we have not found, the echo of a tune we have not heard, news from a country we have never yet visited."

I am fully aware that music and nature are subjective experiences, that a Japanese Shintoist draws different conclusions from nature, that a moonstruck lover may listen to Bach's Wedding Cantata thinking only of his beloved, not of Christ. And yet, nature and art are also manifestations of God's grace. I can take to them the objective content I derive from revelation and let them describe the concepts. Without nature and art, I could hardly relate to awe and glory and joy. With them, I can better respond to such concepts as estrangement, redemption and, finally, resurrection.

CHAPTER NINE

The Music of God

I AM leaning back in a padded seat listening to a speaker recite well-worn words: "I believe in one God, the Father almighty, maker of heaven and earth and of all things visible and invisible. And in one Lord Jesus Christ, the only-begotten Son of God, begotten of his Father before all worlds, God of God, Light of Light, very God of very God, begotten, not made, being of one substance with the Father. . . ." The words drone on, a repetition of the familiar Nicene Creed, words that once stirred heated debate and massive church councils but which, encrusted with the barnacles of time, today normally elicit ritualistic mumbling or a stifled yawn.

Yet when the speaker finishes, the audience erupts into vigorous cheering. Some stomp the floor, some shout "Bravo!" and a few even whistle through their fingers. I look around me. These are not charismatics at a prophecy rally; they are stockbrokers, lawyers, executives, and society figures, all of whom have forked over at least ten dollars to hear the Nicene Creed. For the most part, they fail to see the irony that looms large to me: half-empty churches stand throughout Chicago where scarcely a stray "Amen!" (let alone wild applause) is heard, while these non-religious types pack out Orchestra Hall to hear Beethoven's *Missa Solemnis*.

The "speaker" in this case, if I have misled you, is the Chicago

Symphony Chorus and its featured soloists. But they are faithfully rendering the words handed down by the Council of Nicea in A.D. 325. Those same words, as interpreted by Mozart and Haydn or linguistically adapted by Brahms or Berlioz, are often repeated by skilled professionals in every major city in the Western world.

I know a few musicians, and would not intimate that they perform the clergy function in any willing sense. Fortunately for the unbelievers of the Chorus these highly charged words of grace are neatly packaged in rhythmic Latin phrases that glissade safely off the tongue. Yet as I watch, something approaching miracle seems to occur. A Jewish tenor on the third row, who stiffened up for this performance with three Manhattans and a pack of Camels, who gives not a rip for "the only begotten Son of God," whose chin is marked with styptic pencil and collar flecked with blood from a hasty shave—that tenor's face is transformed. Harshness drains from it; he sucks a deep breath of hope and release from the anxious world offstage and belts out "Agnus dei, Agnus dei" ("Lamb of God, who takest away the sins of the world, have mercy upon us") as though it is the one true plea he has ever made. Perhaps, for a moment, he does mean it.

Perhaps crusty old Beethoven, who, it is said, angrily shook a fist at the thundering heavens before relaxing into death, meant the words as he rolled them over and over in his mind, searching out the most profound way of communicating them. The music, so powerful a carrier of thoughts too unearthly to be fully expressed, assumes its own power, possessing composer, conductor, performers, audience. For a few hours, performers' thoughts about the union wage scale and post-performance parties, as well as my own concerns about a day filled with deadlines and jangling telephones, yield to a sublime contemplation of the unfathomable.

I am not alone—even hardened music critics are vulnerable. Reviewing the Chicago Symphony's recent recording of Brahms' *German Requiem*, Heuwell Tircuit of the *San Francisco Chronicle* wrote, "The performance is divine (in several senses). It constitutes an overpowering experience, one which is not only technically and stylistically perfect, but moving in an uncanny, religious way. When the chorus sings of 'The living Christ,' even an atheist can believe in Him."

After reading scores of articles decrying Western civilization and the economic structure that fostered Beethoven and Mozart, and others lamenting the production of computer disks, plastics, and the internal combustion engine, I would offer a deeply felt vote of gratitude for music and the technology that makes it democratically available.

When we total the dollars per hour of gospel preached across the National Religious Broadcasters' airwaves or the attendance in Sunday morning services, do we somehow forget the stunning impact of these monuments to a living Christ voiced by history's musical geniuses?

While I have my doubts about the neutron bomb, the Concorde, and a hand-held television, I am daily blessed by an ability shared by no generation in history: I can invite into my study the Munich Bach Choir or the Concertgebouw Orchestra. I can sit before my speakers and listen transfixed, as did the European gentry who commissioned these works for their great halls and private chapels. Or, I can turn down the volume and use it as background music, even as I write these words.

As music, no one questions the value of the enduring religious works of Mozart, Handel or Bach. But what of their value as a reflection of the personal faith of the composers? Were they indeed intended as a testimony to deep religious sentiments?

The answer, of course, varies with each composer. A few lived disciplined lives of humble spirituality, best exemplified by pious Cesar Frank and Anton Bruckner. The latter especially wrote his works to reflect his belief that God is good and that everything we do should honor him. While hard at work on his Tenth Symphony, he remarked to Gustav Mahler, "Now I have to work very hard. . . . Otherwise I will not pass before God, before whom I shall soon stand. He will say 'Why else have I given you talent, than that you should sing my praise and glory? But you have accomplished much too little.' " Bruckner at first evoked the scorn of his University students for his humble faith. Clad in a rural jacket from his native Upper Austria, with an oversized head and wrinkled face, he would abruptly stop his lectures when bells sounded from a nearby church. There on the classroom floor he would kneel and pray before resuming his lecture. Few, however, failed to come away impressed with his devout sincerity and the cathedrallike music of belief he produced.

Two other famous composers, Handel and Mendelssohn, served almost as evangelists, memorializing great biblical stories and themes in colorfully staged epics. Handel created twenty such oratorios, including *Saul, Israel in Egypt, Jeptha,* and probably the most performed classical piece of all time, *The Messiah.* He treated Bible stories as operas, infusing them with tension and drama. Handel's audience wept openly when in *Samson* the lead character cried out, "Total eclipse—no sun! All dark amid the blaze of noon!"; the elderly Handel himself was standing on stage, totally blind.

Mendelssohn contributed two oratorios, *St. Paul* and *Elijah,* as well as two delightful but seldom heard religious symphonies: *Hymn of Praise,* centered on the hymn "Now Thank We All Our God," and *The Reformation Symphony* constructed on the great hymns of the Protestant Reformation. Because of a cruel twist of history, Mendelssohn is not performed often today, due in part to Hitler's program to rid the concert stage of Jewish influence (though Felix's grandfather Moses was a Jewish philosopher, Felix and his father converted to Christianity).

Two orthodox Catholics, Mozart and Haydn, produced volumes of church music, but admittedly they drifted toward religious themes mainly for economic reasons—commissions for special church events made it worthwhile. Neither could be described as mystical; yet Mozart was so moved by the *Requiem Mass* he was working on until his death that his doctor sought to take the manuscript from him lest he become too agitated.

Profound religious music has even flowed from the pens of men whose lives were decidedly irreligious. Consider Tchaikovsky, an unhappy, paranoid homosexual who drank too much and yet somehow gave us a remarkably rich setting of "The Lord's Prayer." Or Brahms, raised in brothels and exhibiting no personal piety, who came up with the brilliant *German Requiem,* which enfolds phrases from Luther's Bible with music so fitting it seems as if the words were created just for his melodic setting.

Beethoven wrote few religious works, but both he and his successor Mahler struggled with issues vocalized by Mahler: "Whence do we come? Whither does our road take us? Why am I made to feel that I am free while yet I am constrained within my character, as in a prison? What is the object of toil and sorrow? How am I to understand the cruelty and malice in the creations of a kind God? Will the meaning of life be finally revealed by death?" However, musically the two asked these questions in dramatically different ways: Beethoven shook a titanic fist at the heavens; Mahler wrung his hands in despairing *angst*.

Religious music has consistently called the great composers to their highest artistic achievements. Of his hundreds of works, Beethoven only wrote two masses; yet he asserted the *Missa Solemnis* was his greatest composition ever. The not-so-religious, such as Brahms and Schubert, as well as composers on the church payroll, found unequalled inspiration in Christian themes.

Part of the reason lies in the implicit challenge of rendering themes that had been attempted by nearly every composer. Imagine the task of giving novel treatment to a text so devoid of startling literary images as the Nicene Creed. Palestrina churned out ninety-three such masses. Those who followed him agonized over how to express the familiar in startling, arresting ways. Like Olympians, each competed with the great composers who had preceded him.

I believe the real secret, though, must be found in the implicit depth of those Christian themes. In contrast, during its recent twenty-fifth anniversary, the United Nations commissioned a composer to write a piece entitled "To Posterity." Fresh music can come from small thoughts—occasionally a good piece surfaces from all the current drivel extolling teenage love, for example. But give a genius like Beethoven a concept such as "God of God, Light of Light, very God of very God" or assign Handel the surrealistic setting of "Worthy is the Lamb" in Revelation 5

. . . and you can begin to understand what has ignited music through the centuries.

A case can be made (and is made by Francis Schaeffer) for the theory that music would never have reached its glorious zenith in Western civilization without the combustive energy of Christian themes. I will leave that question to the theorists. I do know, however, that when I read Revelation 5 and then drop the needle on Handel's version, chills race up my spine. Music short-circuits the senses with a direct pathway into human emotion. My beliefs about God and grace and redemption are transfigured by the creative products of musical geniuses who plumbed those same wild, liberating concepts.

Above all others, one man symbolizes the perfect blending of musical and religious ideals. I refer, of course, to Johann Sebastian Bach, father of most major developments in Western music. What other figure has earned a cover portrait on *Time* magazine 250 years after his birth? Essayist Lewis Thomas was asked what composer he would choose to represent earth in interplanetary communication. His reply: "I would vote for Bach, streamed out into space over and over again. We would be bragging, of course, but it is surely excusable for us to put the best possible face on at the beginning of such an acquaintance. We can tell the harder truths later."

Born in the shadow of the Wartburg castle where Luther translated the Bible into German, Bach became the single composer most identified with the church, in his case the Lutheran Church. Bach was no saint: he was always offending students and opposing any authority who restricted his musical freedoms. But he had a clear goal. The purpose of his music, he said, "should be none else but the glory of God and the recreation of the mind." Bach attacked this goal with an insatiable thirst for perfection and a formidable knowledge of the Bible (he possessed an impressively large ecclesiastical library). He wrote as though, not a wealthy patron, but God himself was scrutinizing every note and phrase, beginning most manuscripts with the abbreviation *JJ* ("Jesus, help") and ending with *SDG—Soli Deo Gloria* ("To God alone the glory").

Bach's 295 church cantatas (two-thirds of which have survived) range from meditations on the relationship between

Christ and his Bride the Church to exultant celebrations of the final resurrection. In his last days he could confidently dictate this message: "Come, sweetest death, come blessed rest and take my hand and gently lead me on." While literally at the edge of death he dictated one last cantata to which he gave the superscription "With This I Step Before Thy Throne."

Of Bach's most important works *The Passion According to St. Matthew* is generally acclaimed as the greatest choral work ever written in German. It received one performance in Bach's day, caused little stir and lay unperformed for exactly 100 years. Then in 1829 Felix Mendelssohn obtained a copy of the magnificent manuscript from his teacher, who had allegedly bought the original from a cheese merchant using worthless manuscript pages to wrap cheese. Mendelssohn staged a revival of *The Passion*, unleashing a tidal wave of enthusiasm for Bach that has never ebbed. Before he had finished preparing the work for performance, the twenty-year-old Mendelssohn had been converted to faith in Christ.

I heard that great work in a summer concert by The Chicago Symphony Orchestra and Chorus at Ravinia Park near Chicago. Three thousand people gathered in the park for the four-hour performance. Once again I was struck by the irony of that crowd: upper-class patrons, bedecked in evening finery, dining by candlelight on Ravinia's spacious grounds, balanced by a strong contingent of the scruffy blue jean set. Chicago's North Shore Jewish population was liberally sprinkled throughout. All these listened enraptured to a forthright retelling of Jesus' crucifixion adapted from Matthew's Gospel.

Five times in the performance the entire choir sang the haunting refrain from which the hymn "O Sacred Head Now Wounded" is taken.

The scene was as far removed from that dusty, bloody night on Calvary as any I can imagine. Yet somehow the master had weaved his spell. Paid performers in evening gowns and tuxedos rendered the agony and horror of that dark day, as well as its profound significance for all mankind, far better than any heavy breathing Southern evangelist macabrely describing nailprints and thorn marks.

Who knows what impact the performance had? I know of no

church revivals sparked by classical music. But in me, a believer, the painstaking care invested by music's greatest mind in expressing the one event that split history in two found reward. C. S. Lewis referred to great art as the "drippings of grace" which can awaken in us a thirst for the true Object. Under the right master, those drippings can become a flood of God's presence. *SDG*.

I debated a long time before writing this next chapter. A Christian author critiquing Christian writing treads a treacherous path. On the one side are Christian writers, many of them friends, who may take offense; on the other are fellow-critics who may justifiably use my ammunition to take shots at my own work.

And yet we have been too easy on ourselves for too long. Could the nonreligious press be ignoring Christian books partly because of our failure to take ourselves seriously enough? If we would police ourselves, and apply our own rigorous professional criteria, perhaps then skeptical onlookers would take notice. And perhaps a Chaim Potok or Saul Bellow or Philip Roth would arise from the evangelical subculture.

Christian writing is not simply a self-expression to further our own careers and egos, but rather an expression of Truth and an offering to the Father of lights. It's time we writers realized that the quality of our work becomes an integral part of its message. And, it's time for Christian readers to show concern when that message gets smudged.

CHAPTER TEN

Pitfalls of Christian Writing

"THOU HAST conquered, O pale Galilean, and the world has grown gray with Thy breath." Thus concluded the poet Charles Swinburne about the wearisome effect of Christianity on culture at large.

I can speak comfortably only about the field of writing, and that indeed has grown gray in recent years. Walk into any Christian bookstore and thumb your way through the orderly, monochrome rows of self-help books, lifeless theological works, and personal testimonies. Very few seem interesting or appealing enough to attract readers from the general populace. Those who browse in the religious stores, surveys show, represent a scant ten percent even of the forty million born-again Christians who supposedly live tucked away in the corners of America.

Fortunately for Christian publishing, that ten percent is large enough to support a passel of evangelical publishers and a burgeoning industry of six thousand Christian bookstores. The sales figures are indisputable: three evangelical books placed on the top-twenty-of-the-decade list and several million-copy sellers appear annually. And yet, is Christian literature penetrating culture, or is the fissure separating Christian readers from the broader public yawning ever wider?

I will leave the consumer buying habits for marketers to worry over, but an underlying question haunts me as a Christian author: why should anyone read anything religious? Hundreds of Christian books have crossed my desk in the last decade and, I must admit, after a time they do seem to look and sound alike. I have watched literary sparks flare up in the Jewish and Catholic subcultures, but why have evangelicals produced such mediocrity?

Sales may well continue to double every five years, but I care more about the quality of Christian writing. I have tried to analyze trends in the books I have seen in order to erect "Caution!" signs around the pitfalls of Christian writing. Below, I outline four criticisms of Christian writing, criticisms that I accept for myself, as a Christian author. I do not intend to point to specific negative examples and therefore must paint "Christian writing" with a very broad brush. Will high standards of quality improve sales? Who knows? I am convinced, however, that we Christian authors must strive for higher literary standards for our works to be taken seriously in the world at large. A captive audience will read indiscriminately; a skeptical or even hostile audience must be lured.

Thought Without Art
Too often Christian writing performs a kind of literary decapitation: we render the head without the body, the thought without the art. We allow someone to speak to us with his or her brain only, while keeping concealed the background and context which produced those thoughts. For example, we will record Christian leaders' thoughts about life styles without delving into how they spend their own money and free time. In our profiles of Christian leaders, we give little regard to the stages of development and processes that contributed to form their opinions.

Numerous examples in the secular world should teach us how a person's head can be artfully connected to his body, and John McPhee is one of the best practitioners. McPhee resists the moniker of nonfiction, and why indeed should a category of writing be labeled by what it is not? Preferring "the literature of fact," he has led the way in showing how fact can be written as good literature.

I think especially of McPhee's book, *Encounters With the*

Archdruid, in which he sets conservationist David Brower against the forces that would destroy his beloved nature. Of the scores of articles and books I have read analyzing the clash between industrial growth and natural resource conservation, none comes close to McPhee's artful presentation. He sets the stage by describing the adversaries.

Brower hardly resembles the stereotyped Forest Ranger or mountain hiker: he is balding and, except for a pot-belly, seems frail, with pale legs like toothpicks protruding from his shorts. But he has led the fight for conservation, first with the Sierra Club and then with the John Muir Institute. (And, incidentally, he has climbed nearly every mountain in America over 14,000 feet.)

Floyd Dominy is Brower's exact opposite: a tall, good-looking cowboy who wears a ten-gallon hat, smokes a fat cigar, and spins one yarn after another. Starting back in Dust Bowl days, Dominy devoted his life to building dams and eventually rose to the position of head of the Bureau of Land Management. He and Brower constantly lock horns, especially in courtrooms, as Brower seeks injunctions to halt Dominy's latest dam project. Everything you would want to know about the complex growth/no growth decisions confronting civilization is contained in McPhee's book, but embodied in an absorbing style. Entertaining personalities come to stand as archetypes for the philosophies they represent.

In one sequence, McPhee takes a rafting trip down the Colorado River with Brower and Dominy. There, in the surging rapids of the Colorado, between the gorges of the Grand Canyon, around a fire on the great river's banks, we get to know the two men and observe the collision of two powerful movements in Western civilization. Perhaps McPhee does not include as many histrionic facts about the clash as other reporters and journalists might have done, but no one I have read captures the conflict more graphically. McPhee gives us the ideas behind each movement in an unforgettable narrative form.

George Plimpton accomplished the same result in a different arena with an article in *Harper's.* He wished to feature Marianne Moore, a demure Catholic poet. But who today reads articles on poets, even if this poet is one of the greatest? In a stroke of great ingenuity, Plimpton succeeded by linking her with one of the worst poets, but most colorful characters, of our time. He set up a luncheon between Moore and Muhammad Ali, and simply recorded what happened.

What happened was that Muhammad Ali decided to honor Marianne Moore by letting her participate with him on a joint effort. His topic: a fight with Ernie Terrell. Plimpton describes the hilarious interaction of Ali and the utterly intimidated Moore. The two finally do produce a "poem." Writes Plimpton, "While we waited, he told me that he was going to get the poem out over the Associated Press wire that afternoon. Mrs. Moore's eyes widened. The irony of all those years struggling with *Broom* and all the other literary magazines, and now to be with a fighter who promised instant publication over a ticker. It did not help the flow of inspiration. She was doubtless intimidated by Ali's presence, especially at his obvious concern that she, a distin-guished poet, was having such a hard time holding up her side. In his mind speed of delivery was very much a qualification of a professional poet."

In his indirect way, Plimpton exposes American culture and its values and the role of art and entertainment in that culture. He achieves that in a holistic and incarnational manner. His treatment is memorable, but not shrill; in fact, he never draws the moral for his readers. The article itself is the message—the implication of that bizarre lunch being the only way to gain national exposure for Marianne Moore.

In contrast to McPhee and Plimpton, Christian authors tend to give *only* the ideas and thoughts, without tracing the person-alities involved and the context of how those thoughts de-veloped. Too often religious books are organized and written like sermons, with an outlined structure superimposed on the content.

Many successful evangelical authors are not authors at all; they are speakers who make their living by speaking at churches and conferences. One can hardly blame them for organizing their written material in the same way as their spoken material, and often it sells well. But speakers who write books in the same style defy the basic rules of communication. Writers cannot merely list facts and hope to penetrate readers' brains. They must take readers on an emotional journey to hold their attention. People do not read the same way they listen, and a book-speech is effective only among an audience previously committed to agree with the material. It cannot reach out to a noncaptive audience such as a world skeptical of Christian ideas. That requires books created according to the rules of written communication.

An author cannot captivate an audience with his or her own personal magnetism as a speaker can. Authors must use such techniques as a gripping narrative style, well-placed anecdotes, suspense, and a structure that compels a reader to follow the train of thought. To a diverse audience, ideas come across best when they are embodied and live within a visual, imaginable context.

Of contemporary Christian writers working in the field of "nonfiction," I know of no one who finds more consistent artistic success than Frederick Buechner. He tackles formidable tasks in his choice of material: retold Bible stories (*Peculiar Treasures*); jazzed-up theology (*Wishful Thinking*); sermons (*Magnificent Defeat, The Hungering Dark*); and even a fictionalized biography of a saint (*Godric*). In each of these genres Buechner applies his sharply honed novelist's skills, and one cannot fault the books for didacticism or boredom.

In *Telling The Truth*, Buechner constructed a book around one thematic sentence: "The gospel is, in some ways, like a tragedy, a comedy and a fairy tale." It covers old ground but, through wise use of images and allusions to literary sources as disparate as *King Lear* and *The Wizard of Oz*, Buechner makes the basic facts of the gospel glow as though he has just discovered the truth in a pottery jar in the Middle East.

Is it merely incidental that some of the most effective Christian apologists in this century—C. S. Lewis, Dorothy Sayers, George MacDonald, G. K. Chesterton—drank deeply at the well of fiction? There, they learned the need to construct even their more theological works with the flair of a novelist.

Supernature Without Nature
G. K. Chesterton proposed a theory to explain the Dark Ages, that wasteland of painting, music, writing, and the other arts.

Could they, he asked, be a necessary interlude after the Roman and Greek defilement and before the discovery of the true Romance? Nature had, in fact, been spoiled. "It was no good telling such people to have a natural religion full of stars and flowers. There was not even a flower or a star that had not been stained. They had to go into the desert, the monasteries, where they could find no flowers or even into the cavern where they could see no stars. . . . Pan was nothing but panic. Venus was nothing but venereal vice."

Gradually against this gray background beauty began to appear, something fresh and delicate. In St. Francis of Assisi, the flowers and stars recovered their first innocence, fire and water were deemed worthy to be the brother and sister of a saint. The purge of paganism was complete at last, and Christians began to rediscover nature with a rush. The greatest blossoming of art in all of history, the Renaissance, immediately followed.

Several centuries later, however, the scientific revolution sent new shock waves through the church, from which we have not yet recovered. Nature and supernature split apart. The church abandoned nature to the physicists and geologists and biologists, retreating to the more limited purlieu of theological speculation. The scientists, in turn, abandoned the supernatural to the church and the paranormalists.

Too often today Christian writers tiptoe around God's creation; it is simply "matter," unworthy of the attention granted supernatural issues. (Similarly, says Jacques Ellul, science avoids questions of supernature to such an extent that it puts on blinders and severely restricts intellectual thought.) It is time for Christian writers to rediscover our natural environment and the characteristics of true humanity. By avoiding nature we divorce ourselves from the greatest images and carriers of supernature, and our writing loses its chief advantage, the ability to mimic creation. When Tolstoy describes spring, the wonder of tiny flowers poking up through the thawing tundra, he invests in it the same exuberance and significance that he gives to a description of Christian conversion. It too is an expression of God's world. As a result, both passages stir up the feeling of longing in a sensitive reader. People live in the world of nature;

we must first affirm that and plumb its meaning before leading them on to supernature.

Recently some fine authors have led the way in attempting to reveal nature as a carrier for supernature. Annie Dillard's *Pilgrim at Tinker Creek* was a landmark in that genre. Lewis Thomas applies the same approach but from a less explicitly religious viewpoint. Response to these two authors demonstrates the hunger in readers for a more holistic approach to the world. Nature and supernature are not two separate worlds; they are different expressions of the same reality, and effective writing must deal with both.

In a brief passage, Pablo Neruda shows what can be done with the subject of writing itself, the choice of words as carriers of expression:

> You can say anything you want, yes sir, but it is the words that sing; they soar and descend. I bow to them, I love them, I cling to them, I run them down, I bite into them, I melt them down. I love words so much: the unexpected ones; the ones I wait for greedily are stalked until, suddenly, they drop. Vowels I love: they glitter like colored stones, they leap like silver fish. They are foam, thread, metal, dew. I run after certain words. They are so beautiful I want to fit them all into my poem. I catch them in mid-flight as they buzz past. I trap them, clean them, peel them. I set myself in front of a dish: they have a crystalline texture to me: vibrant, ivory, vegetable, oily, like fruit, like algae, like agate, like olive. And then I stir them, I shake them, I drink them, I gulp them down, I garnish them, I let them go. I leave them in my poem like stalactites, like slivers of polished wood, like coal, pickings from a ship wreck, gifts from the waves. Everything exists in the word.

Such enthusiasm for words should spill over into the whole process of presenting both the natural and supernatural. The concept of creation is, at heart, a Christian concept. That thought did not exist among the Greeks, who instead used the word *techna,* from which we derive our word "technological." The great Greek poets and playwrights thought in terms of arranging or manufacturing their works; they had no model of divine *creatio ex nihilo* to mimic. It staggers me that we Christians so blithely forfeit our opportunity to explore that magnificently created world. We fly instead to a supernatural world so far elevated from our fringe readers that they cannot possibly make the leap.

Conversely, when we discuss the realm of the supernatural, we must do so with unflinching realism. An article I read recently described a solemn vigil in which the author, standing before the Washington monument, listened reverentially as someone read aloud the names of thousands of those killed by the Hiroshima bomb. He was participating in some anniversary sponsored by an antiwar group. He described a terrible dilemma: while doing his very best to concentrate on the horrible immolation of Hiroshima's victims, his mind ineluctably dragged him back to the more immediate pain of his aching feet. His weak arches could not bear this vigil. Similarly, why cannot we be honest about such spiritual acts as praying and truly portray the dilemma of unholy people performing holy acts while contemplating fallen arches, twitching eyelids, and wobbly knees?

In short, we need a more supernatural awareness of the natural world and a deeper natural sensitivity to the supernatural world. In our art the two must come together, and fuse.

Action Without Tension
Sometimes when I read Christian books, especially in the fields of fiction and biography, I have a suspicion that characters have been strangely lobotomized. It's as if an invasion of body snatchers has sucked out the humanity I know and replaced it with a sterilized imitation. Just as a lobotomy flattens out emotional peaks and valleys, Christian writers can tend to safely reduce life's tensions and strains to a more acceptable level.

A biblical book such as *Jeremiah* or *Hosea* spends a full chapter describing, in graphic terms, Israel's resemblance to a harlot who goes a-whoring, sleeping with every nation that comes down the street. We tend to take those same thoughts and express them as "God is mad at us," or "God is disappointed in Israel." Tragically, we also miss the emotional force of forgiveness that follows such gross adultery. We lobotomize the relationship between God and ourselves, and ourselves and other people.

We express theological concepts without the emotion, the

drama, or the tension. Old Testament Jews understood the full impact of words like atonement and forgiveness: they watched as the priest slid a knife across the spurting artery of a fear-stiffened lamb.

A perverse fear of overstatement keeps us confined to that flatland realm of "safe" emotions and tensions—a fear that seems incredible in light of the biblical model. Why is it that three-hundred-page novelizations of biblical characters somehow seem more stereotyped than the five-page description in the original source? As a beginning, we must turn to the masters of good writing and learn how tension and emotion can be expressed in print. Of modern authors, few excel James Dickey, John Updike, and William Faulkner in ability to take the most ordinary event, say, a dinner conversation, and render it in a captivating manner. As for drama, Dickey can sustain a climb up a one-hundred-foot cliff for fifty pages, keeping the reader's heart pounding violently all the way. These skills can be acquired, but *only* through intense study and effort.

Far more difficult is the task of weaving morality into the fabric of the narrative. We Christian writers lapse into thinking of the world in terms of good or evil instead of the inseparable mixture of good *and* evil present in every person and nearly every action. Earlier times yearned for caricatured saints; they ascribed miracles when there were none. Our time scoffs at miracles and debunks saints. In order to communicate to a skeptical audience, Christian writers must temper their portrayal of good with a strong emphasis on realism.

Again, successful models abound. Consider Dostoyevsky, perhaps the greatest "interior" novelist, who displayed such profound insight into the human psyche. His Christ figure, the protagonist of *The Idiot*, appears as a strange, unpredictable epileptic prince. His goodness, though, is unquestioned, and *The Idiot's* final scene presents perhaps the most moving depiction of grace in all of literature: the "idiot" prince compassionately embracing the man who has just killed his lover. In *Crime and Punishment*, Dostoyevsky presents the darkest side of human nature, but even there the deranged murderer softens in the glow of Sonya's love. Somehow Dostoyevsky accomplishes both justice and forgiveness. In *The Brothers Karamazov* Dostoyevsky presents a truly good man, but counterbalances that character with two brothers. How is it that, a hundred years after Dostoyevsky, Christian literature has, by and large, fallen back into a heroes-and-villains mentality?

A few novelists manage a believable blending of good and evil. Interestingly, these all present a badly flawed protagonist, seemingly a *sine qua non* of modern literature. Consider the whiskey priest in Graham Greene's *The Power and the Glory*, Mauriac's irascible curmudgeon in *Viper's Tangle*, Bernanos' frail saint in *Diary of a Country Priest* and Buechner's tragicomic evangelist in the Leo Bebb series.

Light Without Darkness

Reading religious books sometimes reminds me of traveling through a mile-long mountain tunnel. Inside the tunnel, headlights provide the crucial illumination; without them I would drift dangerously toward the tunnel walls. But as I near the tunnel exit, a bright spot of light appears that soon engulfs my headlights and makes them useless. When I emerge from the tunnel, a "check headlights" sign reminds me that I still have them on. In comparison to the light of day they are so faint that I have lost awareness of them.

Christian books are normally written from a perspective outside the tunnel. The author's viewpoint is already so flooded with light that the author forgets the blank darkness inside the tunnel where many of his or her readers are journeying. We forget that, to someone in the middle of the mile-long tunnel, descriptions of blinding light can easily seem unreal.

When I pick up many Christian books, I get the same sensation as when I read the last page of a novel first. I know where it's going before I start. We desperately need authors with the skill to portray evolving viewpoints and marks of progression along the spiritual journey as accurately and sensitively as they show the light outside the tunnel.

I think of William Faulkner's *The Sound and the Fury* or Ken Kesey's *One Flew Over the Cuckoo's Nest* as examples of shifting points of view. Kesey tells his tale through the viewpoint of the mute Indian who, at the beginning, is thoroughly insane. As McMurphy weaves his liberating spell on twelve fellow inmates, however, the qualities of courage, hope, and self-confidence suddenly seep into that human prison. You can watch the Indian edge toward sanity as the book progresses; his own narrative begins to make more sense. Near the end of the book Kesey slips in an unexpected hint that perhaps there is only one truly insane person in the entire asylum—McMurphy, the one who seemed defiantly sane. At last McMurphy is lobotomized and brought back to the ward strapped to a frame in a symbolic cruciform posture, and the captives (twelve) finally rebel. The movie version, of course, did not capture that subtlety; the medium cannot sustain it.

Kesey's book succeeds because he writes as compellingly from the insane person's point of view as from the sane person's, just as Dostoyevsky in *Karamazov* argued the agnostic's views as strenuously as the believer's. Christian books should allow the reader to understand lack of faith as well as faith; if not, they will be read only by those predisposed to belief. The insanity must sound like insanity, not just glimmers of insanity as recalled by the sane. Doubt must sound like true doubt. In the middle of the tunnel, where one can barely fathom a headlight, pure daylight may blind.

These four criticisms of religious writing I accept for myself. Other Christian authors share my perceptions and are working hard to raise the standards of religious publishing.

Dorothy L. Sayers dedicated one of her books "In the name of One who assuredly never bored one in the thirty-three years He passed through the world like a flame." But we Christian authors must confess to having bored plenty of people. So far the evangelical reading public has been tolerant, buying millions of books of uneven quality each year. But a saturation point is inevitable. If Christian writing is not only to maintain interest in the forgiving Christian audience, but also to arouse interest in the skeptical world beyond the Christian subculture, then it must grow up.

If we need models of how to do it well, we need only look as far as the Bible. Only ten percent of the Bible's material, the epistles, is presented in a thought-organized format. The rest contains rollicking love stories, drama, history, poetry, and parables. There, humanity is presented as realistically as in any literature.

Why else do the paired books of Samuel, Kings, and Chronicles exist, if not to give a detailed context to the environment in which angry prophets were to deliver their messages? Can we imagine a more skillful weaving of nature and supernature than the great nature psalms, the theological high drama of Job and the homespun parables of Jesus? What literary characters demonstrate a more subtle mixture of good and evil than David, or Jeremiah, or Jacob? And, from the despair of Ecclesiastes to the conversion narratives of Acts, is any wavelength on the spectrum of faith and doubt left unexpressed on the Bible's pages?

C. S. Lewis once likened his role as a Christian writer to an adjective humbly striving to point others to the Noun of truth. For people to believe that Noun, we Christian writers must improve our adjectives.

If I had to choose the single most decisive battleground for contemporary Christian writers, it would be the conflict between art and propaganda. For the nonfiction writer, the issue is how to express the Christian message in a structure and style that satisfies the demands of artistic integrity. The fiction writer struggles to include a nonintrusive, self-coherent message in his believable narrative.

Christian art has gained a reputation for erring on the side of propaganda. As a result, novels and especially films with an explicit Christian theme encounter mild condescension if not actual ridicule. Much secular resistance to propaganda appears hypocritical on close inspection, for Christians are not the only propagandists at work. Yet a baldly propagandistic film such as Mon Oncle d'Amerique (My American Uncle), *a gospel tract of behaviorism, somehow becomes the darling of film festivals. A film of that style with a traditional Christian message would be hooted off the screen. Clearly, some kinds of propaganda find wider acceptance than others.*

I include this chapter as a challenge to all Christians working in the arts, as well as Christian readers, viewers, and hearers who experience both good and bad Christian art. The church, once the dominant driving energy in artistic expression, now lags far behind, largely, I am convinced, because of an imbalance between art and propaganda.

CHAPTER ELEVEN

Art and Propaganda

IF SOMEONE were to tell me that it lay in my power to write a novel explaining every social question from a particular viewpoint that I believed to be the correct one, I still wouldn't spend two hours on it. But if I were told that what I am writing will be read in twenty years' time by the children of today, and that those children will laugh, weep, and learn to love life as they read, why then I would devote the whole of my life and energy to it.

The man who wrote those words, Leo Tolstoy, vacillated continually between art and propaganda. Twenty years, even seventy years, after his death people are still laughing, weeping, and learning to love life as they read his books, but others are also reflecting on, arguing with, and reacting to his particular viewpoint on social, moral and religious questions. Although in this quote Tolstoy claims to come down firmly on the side of art, veins of "propaganda" run throughout his novels, inspiring some readers and infuriating others. In nonfiction works like *What is Art?* the great novelist leans toward propaganda, even, as some conclude, at the expense of true art.

Like a bipolar magnet, the Christian author today feels the pull of both forces: a fervent desire to communicate what gives life meaning counteracted by an artistic inclination toward self-expression, form, and structure that any "message" might interrupt. The result: a constant, dichotomous pull toward both propaganda and art. Propaganda is a word currently out of favor, connoting unfair manipulation or distortion of means to an end. I use it in a more acceptable sense, the original sense of the word as coined by Pope Urban VIII. He formed the College of Propaganda in the seventeenth century in order to disseminate the Christian faith. As a Christian writer, I must readily admit that I do strive for propaganda in this sense. Much of what I write is designed to convert or to cause others to consider a viewpoint I hold to be true.

Counterbalancing the literary tug away from propaganda, many evangelicals exert an insidious tug away from art. They would react to Tolstoy's statement with disbelief—to choose a novel that entertains and fosters a love for life over a treatise that solves every social (or, better, religious) question of mankind! How can a person "waste" time with mere aesthetics—soothing music, pleasing art, entertaining literature—when injustice rules the nations and the decadent world marches ineluctably to destruction? Is this not fiddling while Rome burns? Currently, novels written by evangelicals tend toward the propagandistic (even to the extent of fictionalizing Bible stories and foretelling the Second Coming) and away from the artful.

Somewhere in this magnetic field between art and propaganda the Christian author (or painter or musician) works. One force tempts us to lower artistic standards and preach an unadorned message; another tempts us to submerge or even alter the message for the sake of artistic sensibilities. Having lived in the midst of this tension for over a decade, I have come to recognize it as a healthy synthetical tension that should be affirmed. Success often lies with the extremes: an author may succeed in the evangelical world by erring on the side of propaganda. But ever so slowly, the fissure between the Christian and secular worlds will yawn wider. If we continue tilting toward propaganda, we will soon find ourselves writing and selling books to ourselves alone. On the other hand, the Christian author cannot simply absorb the literary standards of the larger world. Our ultimate goal cannot be a self-expression, but rather a God-expression.

C. S. Lewis explored the polarity in the address "Learning in Wartime," delivered to Oxford students who were trying to concentrate on academics while their friends fought in the trenches of Europe and staved off the German aerial assault on London. How, asked Lewis, can creatures who are advancing every moment either to heaven or hell spend any fraction of time on such comparative trivialities as literature, art, math, or biology (let alone Lewis' field of medieval literature)? With great perception, Lewis noted that the condition of wartime did not change the underlying question, but merely accelerated the timing by making it more likely that any one person would advance *soon* to heaven or hell.

The most obvious answer to the dilemma is that God himself invested great energy in the natural world. In the Old Testament he created a distinct culture and experimented with a variety of literary forms which endure as masterpieces. As for biology and physics, everything we know about them derives from painstakingly tracing his creative activity. For a Christian, the natural world provides a medium to express and even discover the image of God. Nevertheless, while Lewis affirms the need for good art and good science, he readily admits that Christianity knocks culture off its pedestal. The salvation of a single soul, he says, is worth more than all the poetry, drama, and tragedy ever written. (A committed Christian must acknowledge that intrinsic worth, and yet how many of us react with dismay when reading of such terrible tragedies as the burning of the library in Alexandria, the destruction of the Parthenon during the Crusades, and the bombing of cathedrals in World War II while scarcely giving a thought to the thousands of nameless civilians buried in the rubble of those edifices?)

The dilemma of art and propaganda is essentially a tremor of the seismic human dilemma of living in a divinely created but fallen world. Beauty abounds, and we are right to seek it and to seek to reproduce it. And yet tragedy and despair and meaninglessness also abound, and we must not neglect addressing ourselves to the human condition. That is why I affirm both art and propaganda. As an author, I experiment with different forms and I hope to express my propaganda (if the word offends you, read "message") as artfully as possible and to imbue my art with a worthwhile message. I embrace both art and propaganda, rejecting the pressures to conform to one or the other.

In dealing with the tensions of art and propaganda over the years, I have learned a few guidelines that allow for a more natural wedding of the two. Whenever I have broken one of these guidelines, I have usually awakened to the abrupt and painful realization that I have tilted too far toward either art or propaganda. In either case my message gets lost, whether through pedantic communication or through a muddle of empty verbiage. Because Christian writers are mainly erring on the side of propaganda, not art, my guidelines speak primarily to that error.

1. An artful propagandist takes into account the ability of the audience to perceive.

For the Christian writer (or speaker) who wants to communicate to a secular audience, this caution cannot be emphasized too strongly. In effect, you must consider two different sets of vocabulary. Words which have a certain meaning to you as a Christian may have an entirely different, sometimes even antithetical, meaning to your secular listener. Consider a few examples of fine words which have had their meanings spoiled over time. Pity once derived from piety: a person dispensed pity in a godlike, compassionate sense. By responding to the poor and the needy, one was mimicking God, and therefore pietous, or full of pity. Similarly, as any reader of the King James Version knows, charity was an example of God's grace, a synonym for love (as in the famous 1 Corinthians 13 passage). Over the centuries, both those words lost their meaning until they ultimately became negatively charged. "I don't want pity!" or "Don't give me charity!" a needy person protests today. The theological significance has been sucked away.

Similarly, many words we now use to express personal faith may miscommunicate rather than communicate. The word *God* may summon up all sorts of inappropriate images, unless the Christian goes on to explain what he or she means by God. Love, a vital theological word, has lost its meaning—for popular conceptions of it, merely flip a radio dial and listen to popular music stations. The word redemption most often relates to trading stamps, and few cultural analogies can adequately express that concept. Blood is as easily associated with death as with life.

As words change in meaning, Christian communicators must adapt accordingly, selecting words and metaphors which precisely fit the culture. Concepts, too, depend on the audience's ability to absorb them, and often we must adapt downwards to a more basic level. If I see a three-year-old girl endangering herself, I must warn her in terms she can understand. For example, what if the child decides to stick her finger first into her mouth and then into an electrical outlet. I would not respond by searching out my *Reader's Digest Home Handyman Encyclopedia* and launching into an elaborate monologue on amps, volts, and electrical resistance. Rather, I will more likely slap her hand and say something like "There's fire in there! You'll be burned!" Although, strictly speaking, the outlet box contains no literal fire, I will choose concepts that communicate to the comprehension level of a three-year-old.

Andrew Young reports that he learned an essential principle of survival during the civil rights struggle. "Don't judge the adversary by how you think," he says. "Learn to think like the adversary." He voiced that principle in the days of the Iran hostage crisis when news accounts were using such adjectives as "insane, crazed, demonic" to describe Iranian leaders. Those labels, said Young, do nothing to facilitate communication. To understand Iran, we must first consider their viewpoint. To the militants, the Shah was as brutal and vicious as Adolf Hitler; therefore they were reacting to the U.S. as we would respond to a country that deliberately sheltered a mass murderer like Hitler.

In a parallel way, when Christians attempt to communicate to non-Christians, we must first think through their assumptions and imagine how they will likely receive the message we are conveying. That process will affect the words we choose, the form and, most importantly, the content we can get across. If we err on the side of too much content, as Christians often do, the net effect is the same as if we had included no content.

Alexander Solzhenitsyn, who has walked a tightrope between art and propaganda all his life, learned this principle after being released from the concentration camps when his writing finally began to find acceptance in Soviet literary journals. In *The Oak and the Calf* he recalls, "Later, when I popped up from the underground and began lightening my works for the outside world, lightening them of all that my fellow countrymen could hardly be expected to accept at once, I discovered to my surprise that a piece only gained, that its effect was heightened, as the harsher tones were softened."

(We must use caution here, as Solzhenitsyn learned. A new danger may seep in: the subtle tendency to lighten too much and thus change the message. *Just drop this one offensive word*, the Soviet censors coaxed Solzhenitsyn. *There's really no need to capitalize God—that's archaic. If you want us to publish* One Day in the Life of Ivan Denisovich, *merely cross out this one problematic line.* Solzhenitsyn resisted those last two requests; he capitalized God and left the controversial sentence, "I crossed myself, and said to God: 'Thou art there in heaven after all, O creator. Thy patience is long, but thy blows are heavy.'" Acceding to such pressure would efface his whole message, he decided.)

Whenever a Christian addresses a secular audience, he or she must maintain a balance between leaving the message intact and adapting it to that audience. We who are Christians stumble across God everywhere. We ascribe daily events to his activity. We see his hand in nature and the Bible. He seems fully evident to us. But to the secular mind, the question is how is it even possible to find God in the maze of cults, religions, and television mountebanks, all clamoring for attention against the background of a starving, war-torn planet. Unless we truly understand that viewpoint, and speak in terms the secular mind can understand, our words will have the quaint and useless ring of a foreign language.

2. Artful propaganda works like a deduction rather than a rationalization.

Recently, psychologists have begun to define an instinctual process of rationalization in the human mind, sometimes labeled the theory of cognitive dissonance. Basically, it means that the human mind, intolerant of a state of tension and disharmony, works to patch up inconsistencies with a self-affirming process of rationalization.

I am late to a luncheon with a publisher. Obviously, according to this theory, it cannot be my fault—I start with that assumption. It must be the traffic. Or my wife. Or the others at the meeting, who showed up on time.

My article is rejected. Instantly I start consoling myself with the knowledge that hundreds of manuscripts were rejected that day. The editor could have had a bad breakfast. Perhaps no one even read my manuscript. Any number of factors arise to explain my rejection. My mind tries to quiet the jarring cacophony caused by this bit of news.

I define the process of rationalization very simply: it occurs when a person knows the end result first, and reasons backwards. The conclusion is a given; I merely need to find a way to support that conclusion. I ran headlong into an example of the process of rationalization while researching chapter 3 of this book, the chapter on Wycliffe Bible Translators. Since rumors of Wycliffe's CIA involvement proliferate, I felt it essential to try and track them down. I telephoned outspoken critics of Wycliffe all over the country. One, a professor in a New York university, insisted that Wycliffe was definitely subsidized by the CIA. I asked for proof. "It's quite obvious," he replied. "They claim to raise their $30 million annual budget from fundamentalist churches. You and I both know there's not $30 million available from that source. Obviously, they're getting it from somewhere else." Had that professor done a little research, he would have discovered that each of the five top television evangelists pulls in over $50 million annually from religious sympathizers. Certainly the pool of resources in the United States is large enough to account for Wycliffe's contributions. But he started from a foregone conclusion and reasoned backward.

Solzhenitsyn encountered a startling case of rationalization when the Soviet editor Lebedev said to him, "If Tolstoy were alive now and wrote as he did then (meaning against the government) he wouldn't be Tolstoy." Lebedev's opinion about his government was so firmly set that he could not allow a plausible threat to it and so he rationalized that Tolstoy would be a different man under a new regime.

Sadly, much of what I read in Christian literature has an echo of rationalization. I get the sense that the author starts with an unshakable conclusion and merely sets out to discover whatever logical course could support that conclusion. Much of what I read on depression, on suicide, on homosexuality, seems written by people who begin with a Christian conclusion, and who have never been through the anguished steps that are the familiar path to a person struggling with depression, suicide, or homosexuality. No wonder the "how-to" articles and books do not ring true. No conclusions could be so flip and matter-of-fact to a person who has actually endured such a journey.

A conclusion has impact only if the reader has been primed for it by moving along the steps that lead to it before being confronted with the conclusion. The conclusion must be the logical outgrowth, the consummation of what went before, not the starting place.

C. S. Lewis, Charles Williams, and J. R. R. Tolkien struggled with these issues intensely as they worked on fiction that reveals an underlying layer of Christianity. Lewis and Tolkien particularly reacted with fire against well-meaning Christians who would slavishly point to all the symbolism in their books, such as labeling the characters of Aslan and Gandalf as Christ-figures. Even though the parallels were obvious, both authors vigorously resisted admitting that had been their intent. Those characters may indeed point to Christ, but by shadowing forth a deeper, underlying cosmic truth. One cannot argue backwards and describe the characters as mere symbolic representations— that would shatter their individuality and literary impact. (I often wounder if Lewis erred on the side of propaganda with Aslan and thus limited his non-Christian audience, whereas Tolkien's greater subtlety may last for centuries.)

In chapter 13 of this book, I allude to several novels by Tolstoy and Dostoyevsky which begin with poignant quotations from Scripture. Their authors selected those verses because they summarize a central message. Yet are the novels *Anna Karenina*, *Resurrection*, *The Idiot*, and *The Brothers Karamazov* propaganda? Only a hardened cynic would say so. The novels, rather, incarnate the concept behind the Bible references so compellingly and convincingly that the reader must acknowledge the truth of what he or she reads. To be effective, a Christian communicator must make the point inside the reader before the reader consciously acknowledges it.

3. Artful propaganda must be "sincere."

I put the word sincere in quotes because I refer to its original meaning only. Like so many words, sincere has been preempted by modern advertising and twisted so badly that it ends up meaning its opposite.

Consider, for example, a shy, timid salesman, who doesn't mix well at parties and cannot be assertive on sales calls. He is sent by his manager to a Dale Carnegie course to improve his self-confidence. "You must be *sincere* to be a successful sales-man," he is told, and he practices various techniques for sincer-ity. *Start with the handshake—it must be firm, confident, steady. Here, try it a few times. Now that you have that down, let's work on eye contact. See, when you shake my hand, you should be staring me right in the eye. Don't look away or even waver. Stare straight into me— that's a mark of sincerity. Your customer must feel you really care about him.*

For a fee of several hundred dollars, our insecure salesman learns techniques of sincerity. His next customers are impressed by his conscientiousness, his confidence in his product, and his concern for them, all because he has learned a body language. Actually, an acquired technique to communicate something not already present is the opposite of the true meaning of sincere. The word, a sculptor's term, derives from two Latin words, *sin cere*, "without wax." Even the best of sculptors makes an occa-sional slip of the chisel, causing an unsightly gouge. Sculptors who work with marble know that wax mixed to the proper color can fill in that gouge so perfectly that few observers could ever spot the flaw. A truly perfect piece, however, one that needs no artificial touch-up, is *sin cere*, without wax. What you see is what you get—there are no embellishments or cover-ups.

Propaganda becomes bad propaganda because of the touch-up wax authors apply to their work. If we can truly write in a sincere way, reflecting reality, then our work will reflect truth and reinforce our central message. If not, readers will spot the flaws and judge our work accordingly.

When I read *The Oak and the Calf,* I laughed aloud as I read the Soviet censors' advice to Solzhenitsyn, because their script could have been written by an evangelical magazine editor. Three things must not appear in Russian literature, they solemnly warned Solzhenitsyn: 1. Pessimism 2. Denigration

3. Surreptitious sniping. Cover up your tendencies to realism with a layer that might soften the overall effect, they seemed to be saying.

Biography and fiction written by evangelicals too often show wax badly gaumed over obvious flaws. We leave out details of struggle and realism that do not fit neatly into our propaganda. Or, we include scenes that have no realism just to reinforce our point. Even the untrained observer can spot the flaws, and slight bulges here and there can ruin a work of art.

All three of these temptations to propagandize in the bad sense increase with a captive, supportive audience. When we no longer have to win people over to our point of view, for example, realism can become an impediment. The Christian public will applaud books in which every prayer is answered and every disease is healed, but to the degree those books do not reflect reality, they will become meaningless to a skeptical audience. Too often our evangelical literature appears to the larger world as strange and unconvincing as a Moonie tract or *Daily Worker* newspaper.

For models of these three guidelines of artful communication, we can look to the Creator himself. He took into account the audience's ability to perceive in the ultimate sense—by flinging aside his deity and becoming the Word, one of us, living in our cramped planet within the limitations of a human body. In his communication through creation, his Son, and the Bible, he gave only enough evidence for those with faith to follow the deductions to truth about him, but yet without defying human freedom. And as for being sincere, has a more earthy, realistic book ever been written than the Bible?

A friend of mine, a hand surgeon, was awakened from a thick sleep by a 3 A.M. telephone call and summoned to an emergency surgery. He specializes in microsurgery, reconnecting nerves and blood vessels finer than human hairs, performing meticulous twelve-hour procedures with no breaks. As he tried to overcome his grogginess, he realized he needed a little extra motivation to endure this one marathon surgery. On impulse he called a close friend, also awakening him. "I have a very arduous surgery ahead of me, and I need something extra to concentrate on this time," he said. "I'd like to dedicate this surgery to you. If I think about you while I'm performing it, that will help me get through."

Should not that be the Christian author's response to God—an offering of our work in dedication to him? If so, how dare we possibly produce progaganda without art, or art without meaning?

To those few who succeed and become models of artistic excellence, the Christian message takes on a new glow. Looking back on T.S. Eliot's life, Russell Kirk said, "He made the poet's voice heard again, and thereby triumphed; knowing the community of souls, he freed others from captivity to time and the lonely ego; in the teeth of winds of doctrine, he attested the permanent things. And his communication is tongued with fire beyond the language of the living."

Journalism presents unique challenges to the committed Christian, who must balance the desire for full disclosure with biblical admonitions to be loving and compassionate. The impact of good reporting on a specific ministry may indeed be negative; the journalist must keep in mind his responsibilities to the broader public.

Christian television provides a fertile ground for good reporting today. Its personalities are larger than life and it thrives on visual images. In addition, Christian television stirs up issues that deserve careful scrutiny by the Christian church and the general public. The concentration of resources in Christian television, half a billion dollars a year, is unparalleled in church history.

I chose Charlotte-based PTL Club as an archetype of Christian television. It is flamboyant, colorful, and endlessly controversial. I went as a TV guest as well as a reporter, which allowed for unusual access to people and facilities.

When a shorter version of this chapter appeared in Christianity Today, the Jewish Defense League attacked Jim Bakker for his comment on "a Jewish reporter." Bakker denied saying such a thing, implying that I and Christianity Today had manufactured the quote. I had seen Bakker respond too often by shoot-from-the-hip denials and, after careful thought, I played the tape recording of his quote for a Charlotte reporter. Bakker's apology appeared in the next day's paper.

CHAPTER TWELVE

The Christian TV Machine

HE IS a skilled Assemblies of God pastor from Maine with a lyrical Irish accent. He begins calmly, "I just want to share a few verses of Scripture with you here, and then I'll be done." But, like a politician warming to his audience, he soon begins embellishing. The story, from 1 Kings, becomes less a retelling than a twenty-minute dramatic performance. His arms flail the air. He falls to his knees. "God will take your nothing-ness and through it do anything!" he shouts.

A crowd erupts into applause. In front of them a well-groomed, smiling man in a vested suit nods his head enthusiastically, holding his hands high and leading the applause, mouthing "Amen" and "Praise the Lord."

To the right, off camera, is a formal living room setting, with a plush blue carpet and baby blue walls accentuated by cream-colored Corinthian columns. Jim Bakker, host of television's PTL Club, sits behind a desk there, shuffling through papers, studying the lineup of guests who will appear as soon as the preacher finishes. His wife Tammy sits off to the side, examining her caramel-colored fingernails and fluffing her hair, while sometimes offering aloud a "Praise the Lord."

Beyond them, to the left, singers dressed in pastel evening gowns are arranging themselves on risers, while stagehands are positioning huge, colorful geometric shapes into an attractive backdrop. Miss Illinois of 1959 is clearing her throat, waiting for her entry cue. Four cameras mounted on silent electric carts—$80,000 cameras, the best in the business—sweep over the scenes, focusing now on the preacher, now on an intense listener. Overhead, a bank of three hundred computer-controlled lights swivel and adjust. And rising up from the stage floor are five tiers of sixty telephone tables, with volunteers manning each phone. Behind them, a globe of the world displays PTL's ministry: flashing white lights radiate outward from Charlotte, North Carolina across the world.

And I, propped on a stool amid the whirl of energy, am one of the waiting guests. "That man is our Bible speaker this week—I've never heard him so filled with the Spirit," one stagehand whispers to me, pointing to the pastor from Maine, as she rustles past.

Other people flutter around the studio, dodging cameras and stepping over electric cables thick as an arm. Beautiful, stylishly dressed women whisper instructions to the next guests while a make-up expert freshly powders their noses. The smell of perfume hangs like a low cloud in the air. A producer hurries around holding up placards, warning the musicians they have five minutes until singing time. He tries to catch the attention of the preacher, who is now wildly gesticulating and bringing his talk to an emotional climax.

Offstage, all this activity is fed into an audio control board which is rumored to be the most sophisticated in the country. Twelve videotape editing machines, worth $75,000 each, patch together the very best camera angles.

Later, at 7:30 A.M. in New York City, 3 P.M. in Manila and 8 A.M. in Anchorage, people will sit down to listen to a jazzed-up Bible story from 1 Kings. It's as if an old-time Pentecostal church service has been captured intact, extruded through machines, monitors, microwaves, and satellites, and then magically synapsed into millions of homes simultaneously. No one went to church to hear that pastor preach on the widow's miraculous supply of oil. He came packaged into their bedrooms, living rooms, and kitchens.

Besides the normal tensions of live television, also present are unvoiced but crackling tensions about the future of PTL. For years Jim Bakker and his show have been attacked in the local press for shaky financial dealings, and a feeling of anxiety pervades the staff. An FCC investigation is underway. Executives have left; employees have been fired. And Jim has been more irritable than usual recently.

The studio audience is well aware of these tensions. Whenever a speaker makes allusion to "our current trials," or "Satan's attacks against this man and this program," wild applause and hearty Amens break out. That morning the host of PTL in Africa flew in unexpectedly from Nigeria to deliver two encouraging "visions from the Lord" to Jim. He related them, appeared briefly on the show, and flew immediately back.

There are few signs of tension on Jim Bakker's face, however, after the preacher finishes and Jim begins chatting on-camera with the show's guests. He is laughing, pleasant, easy-going. He wears his patented boyish grin—unique because he smiles broadly, but using almost exclusively the muscles of his lower lip. On the desk are meticulously prepared prep sheets on each guest, including a list of stimulating, relevant questions to ask them. But, as usual, he ignores the preparations and goes with his instincts. He talks about whatever he feels like, giving each guest as much time as he wants to, disregarding the prepared schedule. Sometimes guests who are flown in from far-away cities never get on the show—Jim Bakker just doesn't feel led.

Those very instincts pulled Bakker to the very top in Christian television, first in starting the 700 Club and now at PTL. "It's not listed in the Bible," he says, "but my spiritual gift, my specific calling from God, is to be a television talk show host. That's what I'm here on earth to do. I love television. I eat it, I sleep it." A good talk show host has the ability to make each viewer—not the masses of viewers, but each individual viewer—feel personally addressed. Somehow, to his loyal audience, Jim Bakker accomplishes that. As many as twenty thousand viewers contact PTL each day, either through letters or the phone. In a year thirty thousand call in to become born again through telephone counseling. And hundreds of thousands of PTL partners support Bakker monthly. Because of Bakker's impact, the *Atheist Journal* named him "the most dangerous Christian in America."

Despite his spectacular success and popularity, Jim Bakker

feels misunderstood, persecuted and unappreciated by the Christian community at large. Some criticize his down-home unsophistication, some the show's excessive emphasis on charismatic gifts and healing, and almost everybody criticizes his use of money. After the program, in a private lunch in the brick kitchen of the million-dollar mansion which serves as PTL's headquarters building, he vented some of those frustrations. He reacted with hurt and anger to an article in *Christianity Today*. "The Christian press picks up material that was in error when it went into the paper here—half truths mixed with lies—and then they go with the same spirit as this local publisher who is an atheist and whose reporter is Jewish. All that is repeated in a Christian magazine as being gospel truth. You have a Christian magazine parroting stuff that has been published by one of the most well known anti-Christian newspaper chains, and that's disappointing to me."

Bakker is weary of answering questions and of bearing the incredible strain of the financial obligations he has committed PTL to. "I feel like I've been pushing a railroad train up a mountain," he says.

He is a complex man, full of ironies. His book, *Move That Mountain*, tells of his youth: short of stature and insecure, he grew up with an inferiority complex, in relative poverty as the son of a machinist at a piston ring plant. Bakker recalls being ashamed to invite friends to his home, an ugly concrete block house, painted orange. After he dropped out of North Central Bible College (in Minneapolis) to marry his wife Tammy, the two traveled together as a gospel team, sleeping in pastors' bedrooms, cheap motel rooms, and dusty church attics, accepting whatever meager "love offering" their host church offered. Those painful, struggling days are etched sharply into Bakker's memory, and now he can't understand why people censure his plush life style. He has paid his dues.

It took a long time in the White House for Jimmy Carter to realize that he was no longer a peanut farmer in Georgia, that every word he spoke, every glint in his eye, every personal taste, no matter how trivial, would be instantly noted, perhaps distorted, and then broadcast around the world. Jim and Tammy similarly made a difficult adjustment to seeing themselves as

symbols in the public eye. For example, they failed to understand the outcry that arose when, the same month that Jim
wrote a direct mail letter saying "Tammy and I are giving every
penny of our life's savings to PTL," he bought a $24,000 Drifter
houseboat equipped with white shag carpeting, two wood-
paneled bedrooms, a gas grill, television, and refrigerator. "I
paid for that boat just like anyone else," he protested defensive-
ly. "I financed it with a bank—there was no PTL money involved."

The Bakkers also drew flak for moving into a $200,000 house
during one of PTL's financial crises, shortly after sixty employees had been cut back to save money. Again Jim reacted to
criticism with confusion and hurt. A wealthy donor had provided the house free of charge. "It was a trifle to her, worth less
than the bracelet she was wearing," he argues. "Yes, I live in a
$200,000 home and I'm not going to apologize for it. For seven-
teen years we prayed that God would give us a home. We didn't
really dream of one that expensive, but God gave it to us. Why
should I be so foolish as to say I won't take it?"

Visiting reporters wax eloquent in describing the luxury of
PTL headquarters. The mansion, obtained at a bargain-base-
ment price by PTL, is tastefully decorated with chandeliers, a
grandfather clock, and oriental rugs over solid mahogany floors.
Bakker's office is paneled in mahogany with a black marble
hearth on his fireplace. Outside, brick sidewalks lead to a Florida meditation garden and a reflecting pool lined with fifty flags.
"I love architecture," says Bakker. "It's my hobby, you might
say. This is one of the most beautiful examples of southern
architecture in the southeast United States. I could have taken
some hammers and beaten the walls and made it look like a poor
place, but I'm not going to destroy it or tear it down because my
critics want me to live a life of poverty."

For other buildings, Bakker insisted on importing real cedar
shingles costing many times the price of local roofing materials.
Expensive bricks were trucked in from Pennsylvania to preserve
the authentic look of Heritage Village. The $3 million studio is
one of the best in the world, and a television tower is cleverly
concealed in the steeple of a giant replica of the Bruton parish
church in Williamsburg.

Interviews with Bakker keep drifting toward financial questions, and with good reason. The electronic church, of which he is an impressive representative, has skyrocketed to a place of financial prominence in the evangelical world. The shift of power and resources is as abrupt and decisive as the recent shift of world resources to the Arab oil countries. The top five evangelical television personalities draw in $50 million in revenue a year—an amount that equals the annual budget of the Vatican City, long criticized for its ostentation.

In 1974 PTL was started with $65 in a bank account; five years later they could raise $1 million in a single day. The large Christian publishers, such as Zondervan, Revell, and Word, have for years been building up solid financial foundations with a sales force, retail outlets, and a network of distribution channels to consumers. Yet suddenly one man with a television ministry can easily beat their total annual income. The headquarters of established evangelistic organizations such as Inter-Varsity and Youth for Christ struggle to raise funds through banquets, direct mail appeals, and personal contacts . . . only to find that a television program gathers in their annual income *in a single week*.

Naturally, grumblings have emerged from certain Christian quarters, notably the evangelical denominations, who fear a siphoning off of needed revenue. Most television preachers, however, insist they raise an awareness for giving among viewers and that giving to churches actually increases during their fund appeals.

What do PTL donors get in exchange for their money? First, of course, is the daily program aired throughout the United States and the English-speaking world. PTL must produce the show and then purchase air time from local stations. Another fifteen percent of PTL's income goes for literature expenses: Bibles, study guides, and follow-up pieces, mostly sent out free of charge. And, of course, there is the overhead of a payroll.

But Jim Bakker's dreams, like those of most television evangelists, extend far beyond the television ministry. He has what one Charlotte reporter calls "an edifice complex." In his autobiography he records that he got the idea for Heritage Village from direct revelation.

"Lord," I questioned, "you've given us this property, what do you want us to do with it?"

Sometime around three o'clock in the morning, the Lord began answering that question.

"I've got it, I've got it," I shouted, forgetting Tammy was asleep beside me.

"What in the world do you mean, you've got it?" she murmured drowsily. "Lay down and go to sleep."

"But, Tammy, I've got it," I shouted again. "God wants us to build a village, a miniature version of colonial Williamsburg."

God had imprinted a blueprint of the building in my head. I got out of bed and began drawing it just as I had seen it. With the Carters Grove mansion situated in the front, the building would be interconnected with walking paths and flower gardens.

Besides the mansion, the studio, and the well-equipped offices, the complex grew to include such amenities as a sauna, a massage room, and a remarkable $200,000 swimming pool. The pool, used by employees' families and visitors' children, is located in the studio basement in a setting of white Grecian columns, arched mirrors, and trailing plastic vines. Its filtering and chlorine systems are computer-controlled.

Even impressive Heritage Village was soon dwarfed by Bakker's most ambitious project. Fifteen miles down the road, just over the border in South Carolina, PTL developed a 1400-acre tract of ground called "Heritage, USA." Hoping to provide a recreational mecca for Christians who had been blessed by PTL's ministry, Bakker built log chalets overlooking a lake, and tent and camper sites complete with cable television and phone hookups. Open air tram vehicles shuttle guests along the winding asphalt drives to shady hiking spots, an Olympic-sized pool, eight lighted tennis courts, and a barn auditorium seating two thousand, where summer television programs are taped. The village includes a general store and gas station which sell PTL frisbees, T-shirts, and sun visors.

A massive Polynesian-style pyramid, designed to house Heritage University, dominates the site. The university started off in grand style, boasting it would serve twelve thousand students in four years, and hiring Donald Barnhouse, Jr., son of

Donald Grey Barnhouse, as its dean. Barnhouse later resigned, as did two successors, and soon the school closed down.

All facilities on the Heritage, USA, property, at a $10 million cost, were completed in just one year, despite work stoppages when contractors insisted on cash payments. Bakker also talks, less confidently now, of a retirement center, a twelve-story Polynesian hotel, a clinic, an Old American Main Street, a golf course, a condominium high-rise, and other developments approaching $100 million. The entire grand scheme is called the Total Living Center. Bakker defends the project: "I know some will say, 'You should not have built the Total Living Center,' but I know I heard from God."

In addition to its luxury, Heritage, USA, also bears the down-home country stamp of PTL. It has as its symbol a twenty-five-foot plastic moose, the kind of advertising behemoth normally found in restaurant parking lots. Employees liked the moose so well that they bought a plastic pig to house the ticket concession stand and hid a giant plastic rooster in the woods to surprise unsuspecting hikers. Speed limit signs are marked in odd figures—17 or 33 mph—with the warning "Speed checked by God."

Such grandiose plans took their toll on the PTL ministry, however. In his telethon appeals Bakker often spoke darkly of the threat of PTL going into receivership. On the air he tearfully warned viewers that he might have to sell the studio. "We're within days of this network ceasing." In fund-raising letters he pleaded, "Unless God performs a financial miracle, this could be the last letter you will receive from me." And, "It will be a sad Christmas for Tammy and me without your help." Bakker was caught in a great pincers, however. As he cried and described the failing financial situation on television, more and more money poured in. Giving never sagged. But anxious creditors, scared by his pronouncements, demanded cash before resuming work; banks refused to make loans and creditors filed liens against PTL assets. Television stations bumped them off the air. Finally, PTL had to cut back from a two-hour to a one-hour format.

While Bakker has his edifice complex and his desire to make a splash with big, impressive monuments, he also has a compassionate side. One on one with a hurting person, he can be deeply touched. When a black church burned down in Charlotte, he helped rebuild the church at PTL expense with no fanfare. When visitors from such organizations as Wycliffe Bible Translators or Teen Challenge describe their needs on his show, Bakker will often weep, then on the spot promise them whatever amount they need.

In the midst of one financial crisis, he went on a five-week, round-the-world survey report to see firsthand the needs of other countries. Bakker hit Calcutta shortly after a disastrous flood. The sight devastated him. "As tears streamed down my face, I cried 'O Lord, please make it possible for us to do more.'" Despite PTL's precarious position, he tripled the pledge in order for India to feed more children each day and to supply a new nurses' wing at a hospital.

Bakker urgently appealed to his supporters for personal sacrifice. It was a bizarre request: the mastermind of a multi-million dollar, first-class Total Living Center begging American Christians to give up money they waste on sweets and soft drinks to help the starving in India. The appeal went live via phone hookup through one of the most lavishly appointed studios in the world. Hearing her husband's pleading voice, Tammy turned to the cameras and said, "Moms in India love their babies just as much as you do. They're going through hell on earth because we in America don't care. Oh, people! . . ." Then the camera panned to the PTL Singers, swaying to music, dressed in lace-trimmed formals. Such are the anomalies of Jim Bakker and PTL.

After his trip, Bakker was so impressed by the needs of the world that he decided to commit ten percent of PTL's gross income to overseas mission projects. He did, however, include a clause that allows PTL to use the fund for operating expenses if needs arise. The FCC soon began investigating complaints that funds designated for projects overseas never left Charlotte.

Charlotte newspapers delight in accusing PTL of profligate use of money, editorializing how their money could best be spent. Yet the impoverished people who read the papers rise in righteous anger to Bakker's defense. "If Jim Bakker got $1 million a year, it wouldn't be too much!" said one, "when you consider the marriages he's saved, the healings, the alcoholics, the dope addicts." Even when PTL's use of money was widely publicized, giving—most of it averaging $15 per gift—continued to climb. Bakker has tapped into his constituency. He understands their needs, and they, identifying with his promises of hope, give him vicarious approval to obtain the best that money can buy.

When asked point blank "If you had $100 million to spend on implementing the gospel of Jesus in the world today, is a Total Living Center—with its chalets, campgrounds, and condominiums—the best way to do it?" Bakker responded first by describing the education that future missionaries would receive, then the retirement section, then the nursing home and hospital. Then he concluded, "People talk like there's a lack somehow in God, like there's a shortage, and that if we build a Christian retreat center, we wouldn't have the money to do this or do that. There is no shortage in God, believe me."

Bakker's belief in God as a benevolent resource permeates his theology and the message he offers his viewers. His 182-page autobiography contains fifty-five specific instances where God responded to his pleas for material assistance or requests for healing. In two instances he "felt led" to write a check for $20,000 knowing there was no money in the bank to cover it, believing God would fill the account before the check was cashed.

He, like most of the popular Christian television personalities, consistently holds to a "health and wealth theology," believing God will bless Christians materially. If you turn to Christ, your life will work. India's problems, he says, are due to that country's rejection of Christian principles. "Theirs is a religious, not a political problem." Religion locks them into a rigid caste system and an aversion to using their cattle. In Africa and India, he has observed, the Christians' homes are better and more comfortable than non-Christians'. Most ghettoes, he says, are ghettoes of the mind. "The gospel will bring people to a higher standard than they've known before. I'm convinced that Christianity is a life style—a way of life—not a religious experience. And I believe the Bible says, 'Delight yourself in the Lord and he'll give you the desires of your heart.' " His book relates one prayer incident where a man who asked for a brown Winnebago got exactly that. "Specify the color of the camper you want God to give you!" Bakker urges.

When asked how this Christian life style differed from the Positive Mental Attitude or Dale Carnegie life style, Bakker replied, "It doesn't. They base about everything they do on scriptural principles. The Bible says, 'Give and it shall be given unto you.' " He flares up at people who blame America for oppressively contributing to the world's poverty, asserting that the original principles of America—such as the freedom of man and free enterprise—are biblical principles which naturally result in success.

Bakker's Christianity is not a counter-culture; it is a super-culture, a realization of the very best that the world has to offer. In that sense, it is paralleled by Oral Roberts' "seed faith" and Robert Schuller's "possibility thinking." Health and wealth theology permeates Christian television.

How does Bakker handle such passages as the one where Jesus tells the rich young ruler to sell all he has? "Keep reading," he says. "Later in that chapter Jesus says everything we give up will be returned to us. What would have happened if the rich young ruler had given all to serve Jesus? I sincerely believe he probably would have moved up in his ruling class. Everywhere we turn Jesus was preaching an abundant, full life."

In television Jim Bakker and his peers have found a perfect vehicle for promises of health and wealth. Television is made for packaged promises and easy-to-grasp answers. Shows resolve life situations in neat half-hour or hour-long segments. Commercials promise solutions, not problems. It is a miserable platform for discussing complexity and struggle, and hosts who try to represent life's complexity, such as Dick Cavett, are eventually relegated to the minority viewing audience of public television. Inevitably, a Christian faith tailored for a television audience comes across as scrubbed-up, incomplete.

A non-Christian friend, who has watched PTL faithfully, mainly out of curiosity, comes away puzzled. "If their God is so benevolent," he asks, "why does he allow death and suffering? Why did the Holocaust happen, or the floods in India, if he always wants the best possible life style for us? After all, even

Kathryn Kuhlman died. The Bible can't be as polyanna-ish as it seems on PTL."

Indeed, Jesus did not paint a rosy picture for his disciples or to the early church. Most early church leaders ended up in jail, tortured and often killed. Jesus warned the fledgling church against temptation, dissension, attacks from outside, lukewarmness, and painful persecutions. Discussing these aspects of the Christian life does not appeal to a large audience, though.

Many viewers of a more conservative persuasion are disturbed by another emphasis on such shows as "The 700 Club" and PTL: physical healing. Some accounts are downright tasteless. A man in PTL's studio audience described a wart on the end of his nose that developed into skin cancer. "After watching your show, I prayed, and it just bursted all open, running down my checkbone. And then it completely disappeared!"

On one show Tammy Bakker recalled a bizarre episode of healing. She had a hernia and was scheduled for surgery to relieve it, but she believed God did not want her to have to endure the trauma of surgery. So, one Sunday during communion she felt moved to immerse a wart on her finger (she didn't explain the physiological connection) in the communion glass. She felt a sudden energy rushing through her, and discovered the next day that her hernia had been healed and surgery was not necessary. In her autobiography, Tammy also records a sincere but unsuccessful prayer attempt to raise her dog Chi-chi from the dead.

A favorite guest on PTL is a Southern healer named Vicky Jamison. A gracious and attractive blonde, she reports that she discovered her healing powers quite by accident. She also claims the power to "slay people in the Spirit": when she touches them on the head, they fall backwards in a kind of swoon (with other guests catching them before they hit the floor, and some throwing blankets over beskirted ladies). She recalls that she was surprised the first time this gift manifested itself; as she lifted her hand, people in the audience fell over like wooden soldiers. Now, people can be slain in the Spirit without even being aware of her presence.

Jamison claims people in a fifty-mile radius of Charlotte are sometimes affected when she visits PTL. Ms. Jamison has added her own unique stamp to the healing process; she sings spontaneous words to familiar tunes. To "He Touched Me" she'll add words such as "If you believe, he'll make you whole," interjecting her music with such comments as "You out there to the left, you're cleansed of your colon. Where's the thyroid condition over in that section? There's a growth in someone's breast over there. Sir, if you'll stand up, that prostate condition is healed . . . and I want to find that upper lip. . . ."

PTL is flooded with accounts of healing from its viewers—twenty thousand in a single year. In addition, people describe in great detail marriages saved, families reunited, and miracles performed. Somehow the experience of hearing and seeing others' faith on television challenges many to seek new spiritual heights.

Critics, of course, point out certain dangers implicit in an experience-oriented Christianity. Grounding faith on a God who will make your life style comfortable and take care of your health opens up several alarming possibilities. First is the confusion that arises when problems don't seem to work out. Christians such as Joni Eareckson (who was not healed despite fervent prayers) suddenly feel the implication that they are second-class citizens, somehow unworthy of God's best for them. Faith is tied to a money-back guarantee of God's protection—exactly the bargain Satan wrongly accused God of sealing with Job. And, if Christian faith does not produce the expected results, why not drop it?

Also, when people tie religious experience to a life style experience, rather than grounding it in objective reality, they seem to make Christianity equal to other faiths that promise the same results. Mormons, Moonies, Christian Scientists—they all have impressive success records, complete with their own stories of healing and financial rewards. Where are the distinctives of Christianity which cost God the death of his Son? Exuberant Tammy on one show got carried away, "This life is so great—I just love it whether or not it's true!" To such a comment, orthodox Christians must reply that the life is not always so great, at least in material terms, and it is worth loving precisely because it is true.

In spite of their background and certain emphases, it would

be unfair to typecast the Bakkers as old-line Assembly of God Christians. They do host a parade of figures well-known within Pentecostal circles and unknown outside them. But PTL also has hosted Ruth Carter Stapleton, Art Linkletter, Dale Evans, Anita Bryant, Charles Colson, Pat Boone, Lulu (of TV's "Hee Haw"), Senator Mark Hatfield, actor Dean Jones, and hundreds of others.

Although the show is not an effective forum for true dialogue or idea exchanges, it excels as a vehicle for expressing personal testimonies.

Bakker is unafraid to take courageous stands. He insisted on Larry Flynt's right to appear on PTL, despite a swarm of local critics. One pastor took out a full page ad in the Charlotte paper denouncing him for hosting a pornographer. He refused to endorse Anita Bryant's campaign against homosexuals, saying, "I'm not with Anita on this fight . . . I think we ought to love them and welcome them into our churches."

Bakker's openness often surprises his closest advisers, who reflect a wide political spectrum. Even on a topic like healing he is capable of coming out with a statement like "Now all you healers out there who take credit for someone being healed in your ministry, why don't you also take credit for the ones who aren't healed—the ones who die?"

In his autobiography Bakker describes the effect of one image from his boyhood church: a large black-and-white picture of a human eye on the wall of his Sunday school classroom. To him, that eye was God himself, and it inspired a fear that "God was always looking and he would get you if you were bad." Somewhat in reaction, Bakker today grounds his approach on love, not on fear or appeals to hell. Though capable of brimstone preaching, he adapts to the "cool" medium of television, smiling, constantly assuring "God loves you, and we do too."

In short, PTL offers an affirming, upbeat brand of faith, free of many of the negative strictures of fundamentalism. In Charlotte, the staff seems to reflect this philosophy. Employees are warm and considerate, even to local critics of their organization.

The explosive growth of the electronic church, symbolized by PTL, is such a recent phenomenon that its impact is still being evaluated by the rest of the church. Certainly it expands the total outreach of evangelism, reaching into homes unaware, presenting the gospel to people who would never seek it out in a local church. The loyalty of PTL viewers demonstrates that there are millions of needy, lonely people whom the church is not reaching. They see Jim Bakker as a friend, someone they can count on to understand their problems. Scores of thousands of them write him personal letters and send in prayer requests. (PTL has a full-time person in charge of the prayer room, and other employees volunteer in shifts to pray for these requests.) Their effusive letters of how PTL has touched them are testaments to the power of electronic ministry.

In a sense, says Bakker, each of these letters is an accusing finger pointing to local churches that have let too many people "fall through the cracks." He freely admits his ministry and others like it are supplements to the church, not a replacement for it. "To those pastors who feel like the media is draining from the churches," he says, "I would advise them to seek God for what they are feeding their sheep—the sheep will go where there is good food. If they are fed in their churches, they probably won't need PTL or Oral Roberts or anyone—if the church does the job. If elders would come and pray for people's needs and the church was a place of prayer instead of a bingo game or a social club, then millions of people wouldn't call to these ministries for needs."

Television evangelists have not yet, however, sifted through the limitations that the electronic medium places on them, and its resultant effect on their message. In television, the consumer is in control—at any moment he can reach up and turn the channel selector—so the emphasis of the message must be on what the viewer wants to see, more than what he should see. One can hardly imagine the Old Testament prophets with their stern message from God capturing an acceptable viewing audience. Even Jesus, though he might arouse the curiosity of television documentary crews, would hardly fit the normal television format; his discussions were too slippery, not packaged right for a consumer society.

Bakker admits television ratings limit him from, for example, Bible exposition. Yet television can offer contributions not available to the local church. What local church could afford the weekly lineup of famous guests that parade before Robert Schuller's, Pat Robertson's, or Jim Bakker's cameras, as well as the music professionalism of Gary Paxton, Paul Stookey, Reba Rambo, and B. J. Thomas?

To people on the fringes of Christianity, especially those with acute personal needs, Christian television opens up a whole new avenue of hope. The speakers and guests promise that their viewers' lives can have answers and fulfillment. To many lonely people those shows glow as the chief bright spots in an otherwise overwhelming existence.

For the mainline Christian, PTL and its companion shows offer an infusion of excitement about personal faith which is often lacking in the local church. Some viewers who strongly disagree with the philosophy of the show are nevertheless inspired by the fresh example of people who can articulate their faith in Christ. Many report their faith has been energized so that they become more active in Christian service.

The danger comes when viewers confuse the excitement of Christian television with the message and the work of the church incarnate. Compared to television glitter, the average local church is lackluster. Services are boring by contrast; the message seems complex and confusing. And perhaps most dangerous of all is the latent effect of television to create a dependence on vicarious experiences. The church on television is experienced, after all, not in a room that includes sniffling children, restless teen-agers, hard-of-hearing grandparents, and sleepy parishioners. It occurs in a much safer, more sterile environment: your own living room.

When you watch a television church, no one asks you to participate in a visitation program. No one challenges you to hold the attention of a junior high Sunday school class. No one asks you to make meals for shut-ins. The only response PTL solicits is a monthly check of gratitude. What better way is there to reach the world for Christ? A member of the electronic church may easily conclude the answer is his cash contribution to the newest satellite, never questioning whether his own personal involvement is of greater value. What can one solitary person's service accomplish, he may wonder, when dwarfed by the marvels of electronic evangelism.

The Bible presents a realistic picture of the Christian life, including long, dull marches through the wilderness, humiliating failures, pain, and struggle. These don't come off well on television—unless they're told as a quick, summarized prelude to the victorious conclusion. The resulting picture of the Christian life as being one of incessant joy and constant success can actually backfire instead. The viewer, whose experience is different, can begin to feel distressingly inferior, as if somehow he's missing out on the magic of faith.

In essence, the electronic church is the mouth of the body, but without the other parts. Individual Christians are linked to that mouthpiece by microwaves, television cables and direct mail—tentative links at best. Corporate involvement in the electronic church tends to be of a vicarious nature.

Few Christians would question the potential of this mouthpiece, or the remarkable ability of electronic media to expand the gospel's outreach. But people can confuse the mouthpiece with the whole body. Occasionally people are so turned on by what they see on PTL that they pack up and leave their homes, spending their savings on a plane or bus ticket to the Charlotte headquarters. "Wouldn't it be better," they reason, "to visit Jim Bakker in person, to let him lay hands on my arthritis, to share in the financial success that seems so alluring on the television screen?"

Naturally, PTL is not set up to handle pensions, senior citizens' housing, marriage counseling, healing clinics, food distribution outlets, and race relations centers. It disappoints many who come because it is not the church, but only a mouthpiece. By appealing to the needs in humanity which can only be met on a local, corporate level, PTL fosters exactly the kind of situation it is not set up to handle. Despite compassion shown by individual PTL staffers, many of these vagrant people turn away, bitter.

In order to experience a direct link with the people PTL is reaching, on my last day there I volunteered as a phone counsellor during the live TV show. I was given a book, *Speaking with God in the Unknown Tongue*, but cautioned not to exercise glossolalia on the telephone. I was quickly informed how to handle suicide calls and prank calls, and briefed on how to fill out the four basic telephone response forms. A blue form is used most commonly, for prayer requests, with a box to check off for each category (alcohol, anxiety, arthritis, asthma, etc.). The counselor prays with each person over the phone, "lifting up Jesus and claiming the promises of God."

A green form is a salvation report which details a conversation wherein the counselor takes the inquirer on a series of steps to become born again. It ends with a written prayer, which the caller should repeat word for word. Each person converted over the telephone receives a *Salvation Clear and Plain* book and a Bible course. A pink form is to record praise reports, especially healings, with such questions as "Duration of illness?" "Has doctor confirmed healing?" "Doctor's name and address?" and "Guests on program at time of prayer?" A yellow form is for miscellaneous requests for literature, desire for pastoral counseling, criticisms, schedules, and prank calls.

My first call came from a black boy in Arizona, age ten. "How do you stop bein' bad?" he asked, then giggled and hung up. Next was a New Jersey housewife trying to locate the song "In the Center of His Will." Prayer requests followed, including one for "a fearful spirit and insecurity," two for heart conditions. Some more prank calls were sprinkled in among the requests: one said "Merry Christmas," then hung up, and another said, "Hey, I need $8." One lady wanted to become a Christian, she thought, but preferred to read the book *Salvation Clear and Plain* before deciding. And so it went.

The last call of the day was the most involved, and the most telling. A lady from California described in great detail a troublesome situation which developed after her husband left her one year ago. Though she declined to give her name, she told me intimate accounts of fights with her husband. Her dilemma is basically a financial one. She has two sons, aged nine and three, and she must work to support them, since her husband sends no child support. The only jobs she can find require weekend work, and she has to hire out babysitters. She feels an obligation to be with her sons, and they become mean and irresponsible when they're with babysiters so much. Yet if she quits working, welfare money ($350 per month) is not enough to pay basic expenses.

Relating this on the phone between sobs, she sounded torn and confused. Her lack of skills confines her to low-paying jobs, and she hates herself for neglecting her children in a struggle for survival. She said she had accepted Christ, but was very disheartened because nothing seemed to work out right.

Who could help this woman? The government? They allotted $350 per month, but her apartment rent was over $200 and she couldn't pay her bills with the remainder.

Could PTL help her? Something about its guests with their easy, confident smiles and their suede sports coats and fancy dresses had attracted her. Even in her financial straits, she spent $10 on a desperation phone call. Yet the prayer I offered for her across three thousand miles of telephone transmission seemed puny in light of her problems. When PTL admirers pull into their campsite and plug into the phone hookups to counsel people like her, what hope can they offer?

Could the local church help? As a Catholic, she felt rejected because of her church's stand against divorce. No nearby church had extra funds to dole out to needy people; none had free babysitting service.

This lady, eager to do right, but unable to cope with the pressures of her world, represents millions with great needs. PTL and other programs like it tap into those needs, awakening in them a thirst for justice and hope and joy. Yet television is limited; it is not the church, and so its help is incomplete. What the California woman needs is some old-fashioned, sacrificial Christian love—someone to be her friend, keep her sons sometimes, perhaps help out financially.

I couldn't help wondering how many of her Christian neighbors are too busy watching television to give her that love.

I often hear the question, "Why can't Christians write great books? Is it impossible to combine the message of faith with great fiction?" I can respond by citing numerous books written in this century by Christians such as J.R.R. Tolkien, François Mauriac, Graham Greene, Walker Percy, or Flannery O'Connor. All of them have written fine literature that, to varying degrees, incorporates a personal faith.

A great irony remains, however: the greatest fiction ever written, in virtually anyone's estimation, is explicitly and forthrightly Christian, and yet goes largely ignored except in college literature courses. I am referring to the novels by Tolstoy and Dostoyevsky. Who would not include Anna Karenina, War and Peace, and The Brothers Karamazov in a "ten best novels of all time" list?

Tolstoy's Resurrection and Dostoyevsky's The Idiot express such moral force that in a modern climate they almost resemble gospel tracts. Most of the novels written by these two giants, in fact, begin with a Bible verse that encapsulates their message. The Brothers Karamazov begins with John 12:24, "Verily, verily, I say unto you, except a corn of wheat fall into the ground and die, it abideth alone: but if it die, it bringeth forth much fruit," a verse that reappears at a critical juncture in the novel. Anna Karenina cites Romans 12:19, "Vengeance is mine; I will repay, saith the Lord."

Among the books produced by evangelical authors today, good fiction is as rare as a snowflake in Florida. Instead we are blizzarded by endless piles of self-help books that tell us "how to" straighten out our lives. For me, reading a book on how to overcome temptation or improve my marriage rarely makes a lasting difference. But the message of a classic novel that plumbs the reality of sin and depravity or love and fidelity can seep inside me and change me in a permanent way. That's why, when I decided to write a chapter on what it means to "find myself," I went back to Anna Karenina.

CHAPTER THIRTEEN

A Russian Mirror

NOT LONG ago, the Public Broadcasting System ran a weekly BBC series that popularized Tolstoy's monumental novel *Anna Karenina*, sometimes called the greatest novel ever written. Christian concepts underlie the structure and message of Tolstoy's major novels, so much so that Solzhenitsyn has concluded this is one of the main reasons Christianity survived among Russian intellectuals. After Bibles were confiscated, the novels of Tolstoy and Dostoyeveky lived on.

Tolstoy has, in fact, been criticized for writing "morality plays," an unpardonable sin today. It is true that he used his novels to express Christian ideas, and *Anna Karenina* expansively illustrates for me a puzzling statement of Jesus: "The person who finds his life will lose it; he who loses his life for my sake will find it." That statement made such an impression on the Gospel writers that they recorded it more often (four times) than any other saying of his. Tolstoy certainly did not intend the novel to be a mere fleshing-out of this truth; nevertheless, because he wrote skillfully about life, from a Christian perspective, the lesson shines out powerfully.

Though it's difficult to apply, the truth Jesus intended has piercing relevance to our pop-psychology age, and specifically to me. But first, let's see how Tolstoy developed his epic.

After a few chapters of *Anna Karenina*, it becomes clear that the novel should more accurately be called *Anna and Levin,* for it contains the distinct stories of two characters. Anna moves to center stage because of her enchanting power and the web of intrigue and self-deception she spins around her adulterous affair. But always the camera shifts away to Konstantin Levin who is living out an entirely separate plot, most of which takes place on his country estate.

Two more unlike characters could not have been devised. Anna, a sophisticated, urbane princess, would sweep into a ballroom wearing a low-cut gown and reduce all talking to hushed whispers about her. She can carry on fascinating conversations on a range of subjects with guests while simultaneously sizing up the dress and hairstyles of other women in the room. On a train ride from Moscow to Petersburg early in the story, Anna attracts a dashing young cavalry officer, Count Vronsky. Their affair, its effect on Anna's family, and ultimately its death grip on Anna herself consume most of the plot of the novel.

All the while Tolstoy provides a nearly comic relief to the passion of Anna's life by involving the country bumpkin Levin. We see him first as he's visiting Moscow, madly in love with Kitty Shcherbatsky, a flirtatious young belle. He blushingly stumbles through a crude marriage proposal which she politely turns down.

Crushed, Levin swears off city life and returns to his country world of hay and piglets and farm machinery and ignorant peasants. Yet he is never quite content. As Anna gets caught up in an upward spiral of romance, travel, gossip, and attention, Levin fidgets on the farm. He ought to be happy with his gentleman-farmer's life of snipe-shooting and forest hikes, but he's not. He worries too much about the peasants and whether it's right to perpetuate Russia's class distinctions. Christianity haunts him as he watches his brother die and observes the simple faith of the peasants and of Kitty, whom he eventually manages to marry. Why can't he believe?

In a social situation, Levin is like a large dog in a small room wagging his tail. He blunders, gets angry inopportunely, laughs at the wrong times, and expresses himself clumsily. While other wealthy landowners are enjoying the fruits of one of the greatest concentrations of wealth in history, Levin is off brooding about its philosophical and moral implications. Nothing can make him happy for more than a few days at a time.

It seems at first as though Anna will be eternally happy. Carefree, she tours Europe with chivalrous Vronsky, has a child by him, gardens at his estate in the country, and charms whomever she contacts. Everything she wants in life—social standing, attention, love, adventure—she gets. In contrast, if Levin does get what he wants, he's so melancholy that he fails to recognize it.

Tolstoy's powerful tale spotlights the activities of these two: Anna, who seems ecstatically to be finding her life, and Levin, who always seems to be losing his. If the two were alive today, I imagine Anna would be hailed as a competent, independent woman who has learned how to "look out for number one" and could qualify as an assertiveness-training leader. Levin, on the other hand, would sorely need a subscription to *Psychology Today* and *Esquire*, where he could perhaps learn how to take charge of his life. Obviously, his problem is his self-image.

Hardly a day goes by that I don't receive on my desk a magazine article or book which deals with the subject of self-image. Levin's problem has become the flagship of our age. I must get in touch with myself, I'm told, and I'm offered a variety of techniques (some of which are quite expensive and require trips to California mountain resorts) to do so. My childhood, I'm told, has been a singular process of burying the real me under layers of guilt, suppression, sublimation, and anger. Somehow I need to find myself. I take quizzes to find out my basic personality types. I follow the instructions on how to learn to love myself. As books like *How to Be Your Own Best Friend* climb to the top of the best-seller charts, they awaken in me a hunger for the secure fulfillment this self-knowledge will bring.

After dutifully obeying the advice of these masters, here is what I have found out about myself.

• I am a Southern fundamentalist by background, and that sloshes over into my attitudes toward people. I have shed many of the visible trappings of the fundamentalist milieu in which I was raised: I no longer oppose civil rights, I'm not a Republican,

I don't believe dancing, smoking, drinking, and movies will keep a person out of heaven. Yet, some trappings of fundamentalism I have not shed. I find it hard to have an attitude of grace and forgiveness toward people. When I meet someone, I don't expect the best of him; I immediately start sizing him up, judging him. I am harsh on people who aren't good workers. I perceive value in people by what they contribute. I judge people by their actions.

• I have the personality of a writer. My idea of a fun evening is to sit in a great rounded chair, with stereo headphones blocking out the world, and read a book like *Anna Karenina*. I love to take hikes alone through forests or to waterfalls, where I sit and absorb the beauty around me. Having a group of friends on such an experience would detract from the experience. I'm improving with age, but I used to dread parties, and I still feel uncomfortable in any group larger than four. Whenever I attend a group gathering, I relate to it by standing on the edges, as an observer, watching what's going on. This weakness turns into an advantage when I do my trade, because the writing process requires standing on the edge, objectively evaluating, sorting through observations.

• I react to new people with initial suspicion. When a guest speaker comes to my church or organization, I think, "Who does he think he is? What's he got to say that I haven't heard before? Why does he have that fake, phony smile?" People can win me over, but it is exactly that, a winning-over process. Over the years I have developed an impenetrable resistance to sales pitches, and it carries over in some degree to my responses to people. I envy people who make others feel warm and at ease in the first meeting.

• I am a type-A worker. That is, I prefer working through lunch hours, and sticking with a project until it's completely done. The most difficult activity in the world for me is to blankly relax. I love to make lists of tasks and exuberantly erase them one by one as I complete them. My idea of a vacation is to get out a map and draw a thousand-mile line in any direction, preferably west. Then, with the help of an AAA book, I circle any spot of scenic, historical, or cultural interest within two hundred miles of that line. Each day of the vacation, I get up about 6:30

A.M., zig and zag across the topography until 10:00 P.M., covering all the circled spots, filling my camera bag with rolls of exposed film. After returning, exhausted but exhilarated, I can develop the film and write articles based on my trip.

I have discovered myself, or at least a part of myself. If I extended this list *ad infinitum,* I would have a complete profile of who I am. The unique thing about that profile, of course, is that it is only true of me. The definition of my *self* is that collection of quirks, traits, tastes, statistics, and preferences which are true only of me, out of the four billion people in the world. No one else possesses my exact height, weight, nose structure, and hair curl, as well as all these other things I have mentioned.

Now that I have found myself, what are the implications of Jesus' statement that I need to lose my life for his sake? What does he mean, specifically, when he says I should deny that self which I have been so carefully exploring, take up a cross, and follow him?

A young woman summarized the conundrum in a small group meeting as part of the Lenten series for my church. As we met together and discussed the cross, it quickly became obvious that the cross presents an enormous dilemma to modern men and women, mainly because it does cut directly against the message being taught by psychology. "The Bible says I'm supposed to give up myself," this woman said, with lines of anxiety creasing her face. "But I pay $60 an hour to a Christian counselor who tells me I must *find* myself. He tells me I let people walk all over me—that I need to become more aggressive and not let others dominate me." Others in the group nodded assent. All of us had felt a Januslike paradox in our faith.

Christians give cacophonous interpretations of what Jesus meant. Some would advise me to gouge out my guarded, introspective personality and replace it with one that smiles more often, relaxes easily, and trusts people more readily. I listen to them, but even if I did agree with them, I'm not equipped to make those changes. And reading the Bible has impressed me with the wide variety of misfits God uses to accomplish his will on earth—without forcing major personality overhauls upon them.

I don't think Jesus wants me to deny my role as a writer and editor and go into the pastoral ministry. I cannot annul the peculiarities that conspire inside me, and I've accepted that those patterns will probably never change. I doubt I'll ever choose a week's vacation on Miami Beach, for example.

Obviously, though, Jesus meant something important by those statements or the Gospel writers would not have repeated them so often. After much reflection, I have come to these conclusions about what he meant.

Self-denial first strikes at my basic identity. I am by nature a selfish creature, and I spend my time inside a body and a personality which is unique in all the world. It inevitably follows that I begin viewing the world through a viewpoint, making value judgments based on how things align with my perspective, and imposing my likes and dislikes on others around me. In his essay, "The Trouble with X," C. S. Lewis points out that we spot a fatal flaw in almost everyone we meet, even our closest friends. We say about them, "He's a very fine fellow, and I enjoy his company. If only it weren't for his . . ." Yet we almost never see that fatal flaw in ourselves. We rationalize our weaknesses, explaining them away with references to our backgrounds or our good intentions.

Denying myself starts with a full and repentant acceptance of the fatal flaw within me. Regardless of all my accomplishments, all my sophistication, all my admirable traits, I must come to the humbling ground where I acknowledge I am not different from, but like every person who has ever lived. I am a sinner.

I cannot imagine a more difficult stumbling block in Christianity. It is relatively easy to inspire people with the Christian ethic of love; much liberal humanism is built on similar feelings. But every mechanism of self-protection within me cries out against this painful, renouncing step of identifying myself as a sinner. In that act I lose all the collected aspects of my identity and am known simply as a rebel against God.

Fortunately, however, I do not remain in that state. "Christianity is strange," says Pascal. "It bids man recognize that he is vile, even abominable, and bids him desire to be like God. Without such a counterpoise, this dignity would make him horribly vain, or this humiliation would make him terribly abject." Where sin abounded grace did much more abound.

After going through the humiliating act of losing myself by letting go of that protective pride, I suddenly find myself with a new identity—the exalted state that Paul describes as "in-Christness." No longer must I defend my thoughts, my values, my actions. I trade those in for the identity I am given as a son of God. I relinquish the responsibility for setting my ethical standards and my world view.

My sense of competition quickly fades. No longer do I have to bristle through life, racking up points to prove myself. My role has ideally become to prove God, to live my life in such a way that people around me recognize Jesus and his love, not the other set of qualities which separate me from the world. I have found this process to be healthy, relaxing, and wholly good. All of us will realize it incompletely, but I believe the extent to which we realize it will determine our psychological health. Tensions and anxieties flame within me the moment I forget I am living my life for the one-man audience of Christ and slip into living my life to assert myself in a competitive world.

Previously, my main motivation in life was to do a painting of myself, filled with bright colors and profound insights, so that all who looked upon it would be impressed. Now, however, I find that my role is to be a mirror, to brightly reflect the image of God through me. Or perhaps the metaphor of stained glass would serve better, for, after all, God will illumine through my personality and body.

Self-denial, then, initially involves a radical transformation in my basic identity. I no longer find my identity in my apartness from the rest of the world. Now, I find it in my sameness. I am exactly the same as everyone in the world in terms of my standing before God—I am a sinner. And yet I am breathlessly redeemed and now find my identity as a member of Christ's living body.

That is the general, overall way in which denying myself has changed my life. The theology is basic but indispensable. "You gotta *serve* somebody," Bob Dylan growls in his caveman voice. "It could be the devil or it could be the Lord." It could also be yourself. Redemption is a conscious choice to serve the Lord, and that act is a denial.

The denial process, however, does not stop at conversion. Practically, it can affect me in hundreds of specific actions as I choose Christ and his way over my natural preferences. For me, losing my life has included working in a difficult management situation in a Christian organization when my natural bent would have kept me at home, earphones plugged in, writing articles and books. God called me at that time to do a specific task. It has also meant several hundred (should be thousand) incidents of willingly giving up my own desires for those of my wife. Self-denial for me has included acts of pain, such as seeking out a sick, whining friend in a hospital, and even firing an employee at work. It has meant spending time with emotionally needy people who want to ramble, while I want to get work done. It has meant a constant scrutiny of my use of money.

While Jesus' statement includes self-denial, however, it does not end with a spirit of martyrdom so that I'm left with a resigned sense of duty. The verse contains a remarkable, paradoxical promise. Jesus implied that if we lose our lives for his sake we will find them *in the very process of losing them.*

I understand this best by thinking of the various Christians I have interviewed for magazines. I lump them into two sets: Christian entertainers and Christian servants. The Christian entertainers—musicians, actors, speakers, comedians—fill our periodicals and television shows. We fawn over them, reward them with extravagant book contracts and fan mail. They have everything they want. Yet many whom I've interviewed express to me deep longings and self-doubts. They feel uncomfortable in the limelight, a terrible place for Christian growth, because they are unfairly being held up as examples. They are playing out their Christian lives before an audience.

On the other hand, most of the Christian servants I have interviewed are not in the spotlight. They toil unnoticed in remote parts of the country and the world. I think of Dr. Margaret Brand, a missionary eye surgeon who in India would perform fifty to one hundred cataract operations a day under the shade of a village tree. (I can spend thirty minutes in the local clinic getting a speck of dirt washed out.) Or of Mother Teresa who chooses life among the rejects of society. Or of the faithful pastors in communist lands. Or of John Perkins' workers in Mississippi. Or of the relief workers in Somalia. These people have all impressed me with a profound wisdom and a deep-seated contentment which is strikingly absent from the entertainers. They work for low pay, long hours, no applause. They "waste" their talents and skills among the poor and uneducated. Yet somehow, in the process of losing their lives, they have found them. God has reserved rewards for them which are unattainable in any other way.

(Strangely, we Christian publishers and media people are always trying to push the Christian servants up into the entertainers' category, tempting them with lucrative book contracts, TV appearances, movies . . .)

The Sermon on the Mount spells out in detail Jesus' list of practical ways in which our actions may be affected by our attitude of self-denial. Those he calls happy are the poor, the beggars in spirit, the humble, the unambitious, the unselfish, the persecuted. I once thought Jesus pronounced those Beatitudes as a sop thrown to the unfortunate: *Since you can't be rich, popular, and successful, the least I can do for you is to pronounce a blessing.* I have come to believe, however, that Jesus was revealing a central truth. Those of us who are poor and humble in the way he mentioned truly are blessed.

If self-sufficiency is the most fatal sin because it pulls us, as if by a magnet, from God, then indeed the suffering and the poor do have an advantage. Since their dependency and lack of self-sufficiency are obvious to them every day, they can turn more easily to God for strength. The enticing encumbrances of life— lust, pride, success, wealth, glamour—are too far from some to be striven for, and a tremendous roadblock to the kingdom is thus bulldozed. Without an inflated sense of self-importance, they have an easier time losing their lives in the sense Jesus described. The great and the humble, said Pascal, share the same passions and human natures, but the one is at the top of the wheel, and the other near the center, and so is less disturbed by the same revolutions.

If I find myself in the way pop psychology would have me do, I will someday find myself separated from all other people in the world. I will have myself, yes, but that is all.

If I lose my life in the way Jesus laid out as a model, the net result is a common binding, first with all humanity on the level ground before God and then with the common identity in Christ reserved for those in his body.

I want to cling to my life, to pamper it, make it secure, protected. I keep clamoring for uniqueness, attention, achievement. Jesus gently invites me to let go, to trust him with my life and let the Father care for me.

In Frederick Buechner's words, "Inspection stickers used to have printed on the back 'Drive carefully—the life you save may be your own.' That is the wisdom of men in a nutshell.

"What God says, on the other hand, is 'The life you save is the life you lose.' In other words, the life you clutch, hoard, guard, and play safe with is in the end a life worth little to anybody, including yourself; and only a life given away for love's sake is a life worth living. To bring his point home, God shows us a man who gave his life away to the extent of dying a national disgrace without a penny in the bank or a friend to his name. In terms of men's wisdom, he was a perfect fool, and anybody who thinks he can follow him without making something like the same kind of fool of himself is laboring under not a cross but a delusion."

The PBS series on *Anna Karenina* ended with the famous scene of Anna's suicide. Though she had attained everything she wanted, Anna found herself tormented by greed, doubt, and jealousy. What if Vronsky loved another woman the way he loved her? What if Vronsky only wanted her for her body, and if so, what if her body lost its appeal to him? How could she cling to those things she had fought for? Ultimately, she decided that death was "the only way of restoring his love for her in his heart, or punishing him, and of gaining the victory in the fight which an evil spirit was waging against him in her heart." She threw herself under the great iron wheels of a steam locomotive.

Though the PBS series ended with that scene, Tolstoy did not. He takes us back to the country, to Levin. Levin had been wrestling with love for his wife and his young son, Mitya. Why was it he did not feel intense caring for his young son? Was something wrong with him? He had decided to invest himself in his farm, in his family and neighbors and servants, but still he was torn by doubt. Was his decision a mistake?

One event cauterized his doubts and supplied for him the faith which had always eluded him. A sudden Russian summer thunderstorm came up and Levin discovered Kitty and Mitya were missing. He ran toward their favorite oak tree. "Suddenly there was a blinding flash and the whole earth seemed to have caught fire and overhead the vault of heaven seemed to crack. Opening his blinded eyes, he saw with horror through the curtain of rain the strangely altered position of the green crown of a familiar oak in the middle of the wood. 'Has it been struck?' The thought had barely time to cross his mind when, gathering speed, the top of the oak disappeared behind the other trees and he heard the crash of the great tree falling on the others.

"The flash of lightning, the peal of thunder, and the sudden sensation of cold that spread over his body merged for Levin into one feeling of horror.

" 'Dear Lord, dear Lord, not on them,' he said.

"And though he thought at once how senseless was his prayer that they should not be killed by the oak that had already fallen, he repeated it, for he knew that he could do nothing better than to utter that senseless prayer."

Kitty and Mitya were safe, but Levin remained deeply moved by the experience. In that moment of crisis, his true love for them had crashed down upon him. An instinctive, visceral surge of faith and dependency on God washed him with a consciousness that even he, troubled, doubting Levin, could believe. He tried to verbalize what he had experienced, but he could not. "I am asking about the universal revelation of God to the whole universe with all those nebulae. What am I doing? Knowledge unattainable by reasoning has been revealed to me personally, to my heart, openly and beyond a doubt, and I am obstinately trying to express that knowledge in words and by my reason."

Tolstoy ended his brilliant epic with two paragraphs which chronicle Levin's Christian awakening. They were missing from the PBS series, and in fact from the first publication of *Anna Karenina*, which was serialized in a literary magazine. Tolstoy had included them, but his editors decided the tragedy was the place to end, not this shift to Christian hope.

Fortunately, later versions of the novel reverted to Tolstoy's ending, though it still attracts a barrage of literary criticism. The structural merits may be debatable, but to me they finish out the logical consequences of Anna's and Levin's lives. One found her life and discovered it lost: she was consumed by her own selfishness. Another lost his life in others and abruptly discovered he had found it:

" 'This new feeling has not changed me, has not made me happy and enlightened me all of a sudden as I had dreamed it would—just the same as with my feeling for my son. There was no surprise about either. But whether it is faith or not—I don't know what it is—but that feeling has entered just as imperceptibly into my soul through suffering and has lodged itself there firmly.

" 'I shall still get angry with my coachman Ivan, I shall still argue and express my thoughts inopportunely; there will still be a wall between the holy of holies of my soul and other people, even my wife, and I shall still blame her for my own fears and shall regret it; I shall still be unable to understand with my reason why I am praying, and I shall continue to pray—but my life, my whole life, independently of anything that may happen to me, every moment of it, is no longer meaningless but has an incontestable meaning of goodness, with which I have the power to invest it.' "